My heart is in

Bolivia

I hope that you will ask yourself the big question:
'What can I, as a Christian, do in this world?'
That is the purpose of this book.
Fineke Janssen

In order to protect the privacy of the people in this book, some details, names and images have been altered.
Also, some events have been combined, so that time and place do not exactly correspond with reality.

ISBN: 9798405996882
Written by: Peter de Bruijne.
Translation: Yvonne Sparks.
Design and photography: Peter de Bruijne.
Cover design: Joëlle Zeggelaar.

Contents

I dedicate this book to my dear wife Janja.
Thank you for your endless patience throughout the many interviews in wintery Bolivia and in the months thereafter during which this book came into being.
I also thank all the proof-readers for their wise advice.
Peter de Bruijne.

Preface

Sometimes it is possible to be completely mistaken.
You meet somebody who is very seriously thinking about working on the mission field, but then you wonder whether, in the end, it might turn out to be a big disappointment.
Fineke was such a "somebody".
Maybe, because of my own experience in mission work, I was slightly blinded to God's boundless possibilities when a human is wholly dedicated to Him.

Fineke went to Bolivia independently although with the approval of her church. It was not until years later that I actually saw her at work with homeless addicts in La Paz.
The young woman that I had regarded as a temporary assistant to one of our missionary couples, turned out to be no pushover. In order to make herself understood to the people whom she loved so dearly; she would use the language of the streets if necessary. She knows how to use her gift for languages.

How full of prejudice we are, often causing young people to give up hope of being a missionary and decide to stay at home. Then we say, 'He or she has a heart of gold,' but what we mean to say is, 'He or she is just a bit odd. Why go so far away? Just be normal!'
As Dutch people we like everybody to remain 'normal'.
But afterwards we are proud when we know somebody who has "done it".
Fortunately, Fineke did not listen to all those voices, but she did hear the voice of God.

'Hey guy, wake up. I've brought you something to eat and drink. Aren't you cold just wearing a T-shirt in the middle of the night? Here's a jumper for you.'

They are lying all over the town, often too drunk to hold a normal conversation. They are amazed when they later find out that this tall, white woman who woke them, had left her beautiful, safe, comfortable country especially for them. And they wonder, 'What has come over her?'

That question is the best starting point for reading this book. I hope you will not stop asking yourself that same question. The answer might well be the beginning of fresh inspiration for your own life.

Kees Goedhart,
Chairman of Mission and Church.

'I only wanted to help you, that's all'

'I may be white, but that doesn't give you the right to rip me off,' Fineke said firmly to the taxi driver. The man wanted to add fifty percent to the fixed taxi tariff because he thought we were tourists. In Amsterdam he would have answered back, but not so in Bolivia. Somewhat taken aback, the man stared ahead, while Fineke gently explained to him that treating tourists like that is bad publicity for a country. 'That is hurtful,' she said. 'I love this country and I thoroughly enjoy living here.' The driver nodded and silently drove us up the slopes of La Paz to an area where, that morning, Fineke and a number of friends would go and hand out clothing and food.

I am staying with Fineke Janssen, a Dutch woman in La Paz, who lovingly cares for addicted youngsters and, with endless patience, helps them to build a new future. Each week she sets out with her team to offer hope to the homeless of La Paz in their desolate circumstances.

She has been doing this work since 1989, first in cooperation with a Brazilian organisation and, from 1992, as part of the work of her own reception centre for addicted teenagers.

In this first chapter I invite you to accompany me through my "baptism of fire" into the world of the homeless and alcoholics in one of the outskirts of La Paz.

Every time I drive through La Paz, I can hardly believe my eyes, not only because of the exotic scenes in the streets, but also

because of the unique geographical position of this city.
La Paz is built in a valley of which the lowest point is 3,200 metres above sea level. To the north and west of the town the slopes rise up 800 metres like a colossal amphitheatre.

When you walk through the centre of the lower city in between high, modern buildings, you are constantly reminded of the slums that have been built on the slopes like an immensely high wall of blocks, haphazardly piled on top of each other – soft-red coloured bricks for the houses of the wealthy, small grey-brown clay stone houses with roofs of corrugated iron for the poor. To the south and east the high peaks of the Andes watch over the city. When the weather is clear, which is usually the case here, the view is breath-taking.

But today is one of those wintry days on which you don't venture out for pleasure. The highest housing estates hide behind grey veils of clouds. This morning I even saw a few cars driving around with a thick layer of snow on their roofs. This means that we can probably expect snow when we are up there. As we approached our destination the houses looked more and more dilapidated.

After the worn-out taxi had successfully climbed up the last steep slope, over slippery cobbles, snow softly started to fall.

Fineke paid the bill, exactly the fixed amount of six bolivianos. When we got out and walked up higher, I immediately noticed the difference in altitude. Once again, the thin air played its trick on me and the icy-cold wind enhanced the effect. Fineke decided to go and look for plastic sheeting at the stalls in the street, for when the weather is like this such a thing is of great value to the homeless. After fifteen minutes, four of Fineke's co-workers arrived in another taxi.

They brought with them large, round jerry cans of hot coffee, a number of first aid cases, clothing and bags full of bread rolls. We prayed on the side of the road. Then we stepped over the crash barrier and descended a steep, muddy slope.

'Where are the homeless?' I wondered. There was nobody to be seen, just a dog rummaging around in old rubbish. It was not until we approached a flat, grass strip that I saw a wreath of smoke rise up between the bushes.

A little later we stood in in front of a makeshift shelter of sticks covered with plastic sheeting. In front of the tent some men and women were standing together, somewhat aimlessly.

Their faces were battered, their hair was dirty and uncombed and, what was very apparent in these cold conditions, their clothes are far too thin, full of rips and holes.

Some were so cold their teeth were chattering. Among the adults there were also a few children. A teenage girl was looking for her father and was carrying his coat on her arm. She walked from one person to another.

A little further on, where the smoke was rising, a man and a woman squatted by a small fire. The man was fanning the smoke out of his face with his hands and the woman was stirring some kind of meat offal in a pan. They had fresh, deep wounds across their faces.

I kept close to Fineke who knows what to do in this strange world. When the homeless noticed Fineke and her workers, their sombre look changed. With a broad grin, they slowly shuffled towards the

pots of coffee. Time and again we heard these words, said with tears, a kiss and an embrace, 'Gracias, hermanita. Thank you for coming, little sister.'

Fineke walked to the ramshackle tent and crawled inside. An elderly man was lying on top of a mattress under a few blankets. 'He is ill,' Fineke said to me in Dutch. I stayed seated in the doorway and shook hands with the man. Again, I saw tears and gratitude. He was shivering with the fever.

He had to hold the plastic cup of coffee with both hands so as not to spill it. His voice sounded weak and he spoke slowly as he told his story. 'About three weeks ago I had an argument with my wife.

I started drinking and that's how I ended up here. It isn't a good place. I am sick because of the cold.'

'Why don't you go to a home where they can help you?' Fineke asked him. 'Yes, I'll do that when I feel a little better,' he replied. 'You don't have to feel better first. You can go just as you are.'

He turned his head away a little and mumbled, 'Yes, I'll go.'

Fineke insisted and mentioned a few addresses where he would be welcome. 'Just say that I sent you.'

With slightly more conviction in his voice, he then said, 'Yes, I'll do that, I'll do what you say. In the state I am in right now I can't go home. I help my wife run a little shop, you see.'

Fineke knows these people through and through. Intuitively she knew that this man would not seek help. Maybe he would even die in this tent. The man's voice sounded monotonous when he said under his breath 'It is as if this place is bewitched, as if you can't leave here when you want to.

And if you try to leave, you get kind of pulled back to it.'

Fineke knows these stories. 'Of course, it is true what the man says,' she said later on, 'but, at the same time, it is an easy excuse not to have to fight for yourself, as witchcraft is seen to be a superior power and, according to most Bolivians, you can't do anything against it.' She left behind the addresses of two care centres, said goodbye and added, 'But God is much stronger than any witchcraft, you know.'

I went with her to the young couple sitting by the fire. Fineke dropped down and squatted next to them. They had come from Alto Lima, a district of El Alto, the large satellite city of La Paz, situated at an altitude of more than 4,000 metres.

When Fineke asked how they got so badly hurt, the woman told her that her boyfriend had started to hit her when she did something that he didn't like. Both of them had been drinking too much, didn't know what they were doing and only noticed the following day how bad things were.

Do you always live on the streets?' Fineke asked them. She had not met the two before. 'No, not all the time,' the woman replied. 'We live with my boyfriend's mother, but sometimes we spend a few days on the streets to drink with a group of friends.' There was a bottle between them. With a spatula, Fineke spread a thick, disinfecting ointment on the wounds. Passively, the two let "the doctor" do her work. We said goodbye and shook everyone's

hand. That is the custom in Bolivia. Women kiss one another, but I noticed that, when the men got over friendly, Fineke kept her distance.

We descended further down the slope along narrow, slippery footpaths. We stopped near a concrete construction on the side of what was once a sports field. From here we could see clearly, all over the place, small groups of people sitting in the street or hanging around. From all sides, destitute people sauntered slowly towards us. Most of them were very drunk. You couldn't really see it by the way they walked, but by their eyes, and you could hear it by the way they spoke.

Fineke began talking to a large, black woman in a worn-out, light-brown mac with flowers on the collar and cuffs. She wore old, medium-high heels.
Teresa Perez, Fineke's friend and co-worker from the very beginning, started to treat a deep, festering wound on her shin. The woman's name was Rocio.

Every now and again her face distorted with pain. Rocio spoke softly, with a hoarse, dark voice. The atmosphere was friendly and it was evident that she trusted Fineke.
Later, Fineke was visibly upset when she told me Rocio's sad story.

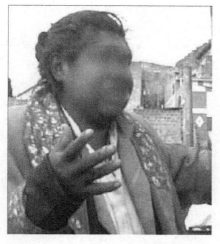

'She is 33 years old and comes from Beni, Bolivia's most northern province, where the mountains of the Andes merge into the tropical Amazons. She was disowned by her family and headed for La Paz to try her luck in prostitution. But because she is no longer attractive due to her addiction to alcohol, she no longer counts in the world of prostitution.

Rocio is an outcast. The place where she feels least left-out is on the streets, among the addicts.'

When no one else came our way, we moved further down the slope. About fifty metres away, a young woman and two men were sitting on a mattress. I saw a teenage girl arrive with a plastic bag containing pure alcohol, which quickly disappeared under one of the men's coats. Looking at them, they seemed totally drunk. As we walked towards them, a small, elderly woman approached us. She was wearing the typical, traditional Aymara clothing - a small bowler hat, a wide ankle-length skirt and a large shawl, woven in colourful bands.

The young woman, who looked about twenty, stood up from the mattress with difficulty. Not only was she drunk, she was disabled too. She staggered over the loose cobbles in the direction of the elderly woman, who removed her shawl, carefully put it down on the ground and opened it up.

To my astonishment, there was a baby. The old woman picked up the child and thrust it into the hands of the young woman, who appeared to be the baby's mother.

I tried to work out the various relationships.

Was this the grandmother who took the child to her own home at night and brought it back to her daughter in the day? The young mother began to swear and plonked the baby down roughly on the wet grass.

However, grandma had already put her shawl back on and was walking away in the direction from which she had come.

The swearing escalated into hysterical screaming, but the old woman pretended not to hear. Then one of the men stood up. He went to the baby, took it in his arms and kissed it. Was he the father? He tried to calm the young woman and take her to the mattress. She lashed out violently and almost fell down in the mud. The child hardly cried, resigned to the whole experience, as if this was a daily ritual. After the mother and father returned to the  mattress with the little one, they received hot drinks and rolls from Fineke's team. It was impossible to have a normal conversation. The three people were too drunk and uptight.

We continued walking. Behind a quarry we found a group of about fifteen homeless people, sitting down. The atmosphere was tense and, when they saw Fineke and her friends, they began to make mocking remarks about God.

The leader muttered something about communism and Karl Marx, but the team pretended not to hear and shared out coffee and bread. A lad of about sixteen showed us a deep, ulcerated wound on his abdomen.

While Fineke tended the wound, she tried to engage him in conversation, but it was clear that he hardly dared say a word in the presence of the group.

In the meantime, from a distance, we could hear loud laughing and joking. A man and a woman approached. The man was taller than all the others I had seen up until now.

At a distance, he appeared to be wearing a nice suit. His companion was a lot smaller, but on her high heels she reached his shoulders. She was having problems keeping her balance.

Closer up, I could see they both looked as shabby as the rest. Nevertheless, he was clearly the leader. The atmosphere in the group changed.

The pair greeted the group as if they had not seen each other for a long time. However, this was no happy reunion. It was the code and culture of the street, the putting out of feelers about who was boss and the re-establishing of the pecking order.

The would-be Marxist was sent on an errand and timidly left. Now Gonzalo, as the tall man was called, was in charge. The whole group consisted of yes-men and cowards. Then the atmosphere changed and became really dangerous.

I could see that Fineke wanted to leave, but she had not quite finished dressing the boy's wound. Gonzalo more or less demanded that a little wound on his foot be taken care of and, when Teresa examined it, he said in an arrogant tone, 'It is quite an honour for you, an Aymara woman, to bandage my foot, isn't it?' She softly replied, 'I only wanted to help you, that's all.'

I first met Fineke Janssen in January 1995. She was then 39 years of age. Adulam Trust had only just been founded and the previous month Teresa Perez had been employed. With the Bolivian board, they were looking for a good location for a home for boys living on the street.

Since then, two rehabilitation centres have been founded, one for boys and one for girls. The team of assistants has been growing steadily and now consists of dozens of Bolivian co-workers.
Since that first meeting the question has not left me, how a young

woman from the Dutch Betuwe area could lose her heart to the homeless and addicts on the other side of the world at an altitude of 4,000 metres.

In July 2002 I travelled again to La Paz to find an answer to my question. Whether I have succeeded or not is up to you to decide. From the next chapter onwards, I will let Fineke tell her story.

Peter de Bruijne, 2003.

Chapter 2

Misfits

It is March 1984. The days are getting longer and the sun is gaining power. Sometimes I sit outside for a little while. I enjoy the warmth and it makes me less moody. I do have a splitting headache though. The endless pressure in my head makes me very drowsy, and it has been going on for such a long time. Last winter may have been the most difficult time in my life so far.

I thought I would be back at work after a few weeks off, but I have been sick now for six months. 'Overworked' - the very word is awful. How often have I used that word to label those who seemed very emotional? I know better now. I was always the tough one. You name it, I did it. But I'm sitting here, doing nothing and it has lasted much longer than I ever thought it would. There was fuss at work and things like that, but I now understand that the real cause is deeper than that. For some time I have been having psychotherapy and the therapist has advised me to keep a journal. Here's an extract for you to read. Maybe it will give you an inkling of how I feel.

Monday – *It feels like I am hollow on the inside. As if there's nothing at all that I want or wish for any longer. Nothing to look forward to.*

Tuesday – *I wonder what the future will hold. Sometimes I feel as if I am at a crossroads and I try to colour the picture of my future. But somehow, I don't think that is what I must do at this particular moment. First I need to get better.*

Wednesday – I find it hard to separate must and want to. I tell myself that there's a lot that I must do. If there is something I want, I feel guilty about the things that still must be done.

These are just three entries in a long series that I won't bother you with. I must say, it helps to jot down one's feelings.

Last week I went to see Dik the psychotherapist again. She is a woman, although her name does not give that away. Dik is very nice and always makes plenty of time for me. I feel secure when I am with her. Lately that's not a common feeling, since I am not often among people.

Of course, my story doesn't start on this beautiful spring day on which, by the way, I discovered something else. This morning I woke up with a Psalm that I memorised a long time ago, when I was at primary school. It gave me joy! I learned the old metric version: "Though I walk in the midst of trouble, Thou wilt revive me". The strange thing is that I wasn't brought up with these old-fashioned Psalms. I was brought up with music though, because my mother was very musical. I've always found it easy to learn songs and even now, when I'm down, I always sing. But before I tell you more about that, I think I had better begin at the beginning. Maybe then you will be able to better understand the situation I find myself in. I will see how far I get, because this headache is really playing up.

I come from a Dutch family in the Netherlands. My father was a fruit grower in the Betuwe area. My mother and father had known each other since they lived in Drenthe, where both of them were born. After agricultural college my father worked as a farm hand in the Noordoostpolder. My mother worked in a solicitor's office. They didn't get married until they were both thirty years old, when they were able to buy a house with a market-garden in Randwijk. Five years later I was born and named Roelfina Lutina Janssen. But they called me Fineke. I was a Christmas child and very small, even though my birth was straightforward.

It was a cold winter and the only way to keep me warm was to put me in a box as close to the wood burner as possible.
My brother Albert was born a few years later.

Mum, Albert, Dad and Fineke

Our house was situated just outside of Randwijk, a small village on the Rhine in the Betuwe, opposite Renkum. My parents still live there. Coming out of our street you can climb on to the dyke. I well remember how I enjoyed the view from there, even when I was a child. Suddenly I was no longer "the little one" but instead I could look down on the houses and the people working in gardens and orchards as if they were Playmobil figures. In spring, when the fruit trees were in blossom, the whole area was transformed into one huge wedding bouquet.

From the dyke, one could look out over the fens with their long rows of pollard willows and the occasional fringe of reeds in soft yellow against the background of dark waters. All around, one could see and hear ducks being busy and quacking loudly, skimming the water from one foraging place to the next. In the distance, the water of the ever-running river glistened and behind was the Wageningen hill, like the dark back of a prehistoric creature.

Over there everything was different. Sometimes we boarded the ferry that took us across the Rhine and then we would go for walks through the woods. When I was a little girl, I liked those high trees but, at the same time, I thought they were scary, dark and mysterious.

That high dyke may have shaped my character to some extent. I like to keep a general view of things and I am careful that no one tries to control me. In my hometown of Randwijk, I've always been a kind of misfit.

My parents came from "outside" and after all these years they're still outsiders. As a child I felt that I didn't really belong. It didn't bother me too much, but it played a part in my development.

Thankfully, I never felt alone because, for as long as I can remember, Marian was my best friend. She, too, lived outside the village and her parents came from "outside" as well. Maybe of more importance was the fact that neither of our families went to the "big" church, whereas most people in the village did. We were

Dutch Reformed and the majority were Reformed. If you asked me to tell you the difference in beliefs and doctrines of these denominations, I would not be able to say.

However, there was a big difference in behaviour.
The Reformed Church members were more orthodox, old-fashioned and less tolerant of anything that was "different". From the day Marian and I started attending the "School with the Bible", the differences were brought home to us. To this day, I don't understand what that has to do with faith and belief in Jesus.
My first day at school was a disaster. From birth my eyesight has been poor. I inherited this from my mother, as well as my love for music. Because school was all about reading and writing, I had my first pair of glasses shortly before starting school. I thought it was awful. The lenses were extremely thick.
The older boys in the playground said they were made with jam jar bottoms. I came home crying and shared what they had said. My mother told me the boys had been joking. It made me think

that being funny means laughing at the misery of others. From time to time that thought comes back to me even now. Whether I wore glasses or not, Marian was still my friend. We were inseparable. We were always together - before school time, during school time and after school time, and also over the weekend, in church.

Because of the strict rules of the "School with the Bible" we also formed a kind of pact against the Reformed Church's rigid rules. The strictness had its good sides, of course.
I learned how to tidy up my things. One morning I walked into the classroom and saw that my desk had been turned upside down and all my exercise books, pens and pencils lay scattered all over the floor. I was furious, of course, but in fact my teacher's actions had some justification. Other things were not so right – like the time I had my ears boxed because I was writing left-handed, which was not allowed at the "School with the Bible".
Only after my mother produced a letter from the doctor

Fineke below the dyke

was it tolerated. The dress code was very strict as well. If girls dared to show up at school wearing trousers, they were sent back home straightaway to put on a dress which covered the knees. Don't think these stories belong to former times. My school made it to the headlines because of its stringent rules.

Marian and I didn't understand why these rules were imposed. How can you possibly tell beautiful Bible stories about Jesus who loves all people and minutes later punish a girl for wearing trousers instead of a dress? Randwijk was too small and inward looking for people to be able to be themselves.

That's why, more and more, I felt the odd one out.

On Sundays we used to go to the small Dutch Reformed church at the foot of the dyke and, as we passed, the Reformed people would not look at us because we were walking in the "wrong" direction. To make matters worse, my mother was the church organist, which they considered a man's role. Sadly, it all had a hardening effect and taught us to take things with a pinch of salt. Marian and I became even closer friends and we discussed everything together. Mind you, we didn't talk a lot with our parents, certainly not about personal things. It just wasn't done. After all, there was work to be done, for the income that the market-garden generated was hardly sufficient to live on. At one time, my father even had to take a job at the Van Gelder paper plant in Renkum, on the other side of the Rhine. My mother then had to do the bulk of the work in the garden. It was taken for granted that we as children would do our bit as well. In fact, I didn't dislike helping.

The atmosphere at home was easy-going when we were working together and it strengthened the bond between us. Of course, we had other pastimes as well. Dad enjoyed playing board games with us at the table. We also accompanied my mother to concerts, after which we would go somewhere for a treat.

My mother was not very good at showing affection. We didn't often sit on her lap to have a cuddle. That meant that an outing with her to a music event was something special.

There was one other misfit in the village and maybe she was even stranger than Marian and I. She was called Johanna. She was always being bullied. There was a lot of gossip going around about her parents. Marian and I thought it was very mean that this girl was the target of all this slander.

From time to time we took her under our wing and then we would give as good as we got. I have always felt very irritated by the senseless group behaviour of the strong versus the weak. For example, the daughter of the headmaster thought she was very strong and, with the help of a large group of followers, she was guaranteed to spoil the atmosphere. She couldn't handle the two of us, but Johanna was usually on her own. It was so mean! It was not Johanna's fault that her parents were in trouble.

Marian and I decided to go and visit Johanna after we hadn't seen her for a while. She opened the door herself. She was visibly startled and seemed reluctant to fully open the door.

We asked, 'Are you ill?' 'No', Johanna answered. 'Where have you been all this time?' 'Well, uh…my mother is ill.' And then, with a shy smile, she said, 'Oh, come on in, I don't care if you know. Everybody's talking about it anyway.'

She opened the front door a little wider and we followed her into the living room. It was obvious that nobody had tidied up recently. As we came in, we were riveted to the spot with shock. Johanna's father was lying on the couch, his arm limply hanging down, an empty spirits bottle on the floor. The man was trembling all over with beads of sweat on his brow. Johanna's voice broke the silence and she sounded remarkably calm in this strange situation. Her adult manner surprised us. She seemed to be in complete control.

'Right now he's quiet, but last night he was delirious and out of control,' she said as she pointed at her father in a seemingly indifferent way. 'What about your mother?' I asked.

'My mother is ill, she is upstairs in bed.' Silence. One could only hear Johanna's father snoring. Then she said, in a sad voice, 'Alright, I'll tell you. She drinks too much as well.'

We had never heard of delirium. It sounded like the name of a sleeping tablet, but now we understood it had to do with drinking alcohol. Of course, we had no idea how to handle the situation but we both felt we could not let Johanna down, just because her parents had a problem. We did not agree with the warnings that our parents had given when they said it was better for us not to go to Johanna's home. Her parents were quite alright when they had not been drinking too much. Then they were nice people to talk to. That's how Johanna became our friend and she still is.

When I look back, I realise that Johanna significantly changed our

Marian and I on an outing

rather protected outlook on life. Outwardly we remained country girls. We continued to do the same silly things and we still quarrelled with the headmaster's daughter.

On the inside, however, a longing had been awakened to care for people in trouble. We grew into teenagers, went to the MAVO[1] and subsequently to the HAVO[2]. We did everything together - we even had the same holiday jobs. Going to the HAVO in Zetten changed our small world we had known below the dyke. There was no more bullying. Young people from the whole region attended.

We were taught about other countries and cultures and for the first time we realised we were world citizens. Many parents of the pupils were employed by the Agricultural College in Wageningen. Some had been living abroad. We were concerned about injustice elsewhere in the world and joined Amnesty International. I demonstrated for the liberation of political prisoners. These kinds of things had never been talked about at home. Actually, I didn't really want to discuss these matters with my parents.

And so it happened that two parallel worlds came into being: on the one hand the continuous struggle to make ends meet and earn a living from the market garden, and on the other hand the wide, wide world and my dream to do something about injustice and misery. Our holiday jobs became more meaningful too. Jobs like

1 MAVO: School for lower general secondary education
2 HAVO: School for higher general secondary education

sales assistant at the local department store were exchanged for employment in the library, the bookshop and a hospital. During the summer holidays, we worked in a home for people with severe learning difficulties in Schaarsbergen.

I still vividly remember that we had to work in a children's wing where the stench was unbearable. I spent a few days in the pandemonium of unpredictable, challenging and aggressive behaviour of young patients. Then I said to Marian, 'I'll give it two more days. If I haven't got used to it by then, I'll pack my bags.'

Strangely enough, I started loving the children from that moment onwards. When the Christmas holidays came around, we registered for employment there again. Apparently, the people thought we were now experienced carers. We were given work in the adult ward. Occasionally we would be in stitches laughing when yet another person painted the wall with his excrement. It was not really funny, of course.

Maybe you're thinking, 'What lovely girls and what a sense of responsibility they have.' Make no mistake. Lots of time was spent on partying, especially during our time at the HAVO. And every now and again we liked playing jokes as well - like the time we went to a house in the middle of the night, took the "For Sale" sign out of a garden and put it up in the garden of the Vicarage. Rumours quickly spread throughout the village that the vicar was leaving. We had a lot of fun!

We also took great interest in boys. It usually did not lead to anything but we didn't mind. After we had been turned down a couple of times, we became a little more careful. One time I was head over heels in love with a boy who liked me as well. We sometimes went to parties together and he was very good at kissing. He really made me feel that I was his girlfriend, even though he had not said that in so many words. I, being a girl, thought that he was the love of my life. I was sixteen and had just started at the HAVO. I'll never forget the day that I saw "my boyfriend" kissing another girl. My world collapsed. I didn't know that love could hurt so badly and, while I'm writing this, it feels as if it only happened yesterday.

After I had recounted these happenings and experiences of my younger days to Dik, my psychotherapist, she said, 'For the first time you began to feel accepted at your new school and your friendship with Marian was secure. Also, you yourself were very faithful in contacts with people. No wonder that you couldn't possibly understand why your great love and overwhelming feelings for that boy were rejected by him in such a callous way. You were naïve and that boy clearly deceived you. Even though it took place many years ago, this could be one of the causes of the crisis you find yourself in.'

Chapter 3

Down-and-out

Six months later in December 1984, I am still unwell, although slowly getting better. Marian, who emigrated to Canada some years ago and married, was visiting the Netherlands and came to see me. As it was my twenty-ninth birthday on Christmas day, she gave me some money to spend on myself. That was kind of her. I still think of her and wonder whether her departure for Canada, all those years ago, continues to affect me in the levels of stress that I am experiencing.

I well remember the moment she told me that she would be leaving. It was in the Spring, just before we had to take our HAVO exams, which I consequently failed. However, I didn't fail them just because Marian was leaving, but also because I thought that I didn't have to do any work for them, like before when I was taking MAVO exams.

That particular day I noticed something in her attitude that made me realise something was amiss. Her pale skin, now even paler than usual, stood out in stark contrast to her straight, dark blonde hair. It sounded ominous when she said, 'Fineke, I have something awful to tell you.' And adding to this anxiety she said, 'You really have to sit down.' I knew straight away that this was serious.

Then the truth came out, 'My parents are moving and I'm going with them.' I froze, put my hands over my eyes and called out, 'No!' 'It is even worse than that, Fineke.

We are emigrating, all the way to Canada.' I didn't know where to look and could hardly grasp what this would mean for me.

Marian was the one person I fully trusted and with whom I could share anything. It didn't really register with me how final this bad news was. It was hard to take it in. Slowly I calmed down and, wiping away my tears and seeing Marian sitting next to me, I realised she wasn't half as emotional as I was. I tried to imagine how nice this would be for her. She would travel to the other side of the world, with a new environment, a different language, beautiful countryside …new friends. Of course, her parents had told her all the details. She had already read a lot about Canada, before she ever told me anything. I think she deliberately chose to wait a long time before breaking the news. At the same time it felt as if I had been stabbed. I fought hard to hide my feelings so as not to spoil my best friend's excitement. It didn't take long before I was laughing again and, during the weeks before Marian left, I pretended I was very happy, for Marian's sake.

My parents had taught me not to complain. That wasn't the done thing in our family. They too had struggled through difficult times. In their opinion emotions are a nuisance and really don't change situations. One had to make the best of life, and there was no place for dwelling on setbacks. Maybe that was typical for the Reformed attitude to life. I don't know whether that's true but I have seen many people my age leave the church for that very reason. Faith and belief were mainly a matter of common sense and hardly any attention was paid to emotions. If you had any questions about faith, or if you doubted certain things, looks of reproach were given and you were regarded as a nuisance. It so happened that, at this time, I was bursting with questions.

I didn't need to retake my exams at the HAVO, for I was accepted at Jelburg without having a paper diploma. Jelburg was a training college for social-educational work in Baarn.
Now Marian had gone, I was keen to leave Randwijk.
Many students lived in Baarn and the atmosphere was much less

restrictive. In those days social studies were the thing to do if you liked counterculture. I embarked in a four-year course on 'institutional work'. I buried my sadness over Marian's leaving and threw myself completely into my studies. Alas, in my college there was no such thing as getting on with one's work diligently. The majority of students simply loved endless discussions, experimenting with soft drugs and being alternative for alternative's sake. It tired me out and I didn't want to go along with the adolescent behaviour of my fellow students. A few other seriously minded students and myself got together and we really wanted to make good progress and get on with our training. The other students thought of us as being weirdos and show-offs.

It looked as if history was repeating itself, and once more I was the odd one out. Although this time it wasn't because I didn't fit the rules of the college, but because the college didn't enforce any rules. Happily, a few teachers supported us and they encouraged us not to go along with the others if we didn't want to.

Many students were spoilt children with rich parents, choosing a social study because of its less strict culture. On occasion, the absurdity of it all came to a head.

Like the time when a whole class decided to play a risqué practical joke. This was during an open day where parents and interested parties were invited to come and look round the school. These students put on a photographic exhibition of penises. Early that morning, and with the help of the caretaker, a friend and I stuck cut outs of "fig leaves" on the photos. Our joke was not well received by the so-called champions of the sexual revolution.

I just didn't want any more of that adolescent behaviour. I had suffered a few hefty blows and wanted to reach my goal as soon as possible, which was doing something for marginalised people in society.

My passion had actually little to do with my faith. Church didn't mean much to me. During the period that I was first living in digs in Baarn, I didn't go to church at all. I had rejected it for now, not so much faith but rather the church. In Heteren, close to Randwijk,

I had attended Bible classes.

I had even been active in a children's club and had led a children's choir. But now that I was living on my own, I didn't just want to go to church for the sake of tradition or to please my parents. If I went, it would have to be because I personally wanted to go.

Eighteen months after leaving home, I attended a Reformed Church service in Baarn. It wasn't too bad at all. The sermon was interesting and the vicar even took the young people into account. To me he seemed to be a person who wasn't scared off by critical questions. A few Sundays later I met him personally and he asked me if I would like to attend confirmation classes. I decided I would go for it.

This was really awesome. We could ask any question whatsoever and the vicar was not easily daunted. If there were questions he could not answer, he didn't try to hide the fact. He didn't give you the feeling that you shouldn't have been asking the question. That's what I had been used to in my home church. In my third year of college I was confirmed in Baarn. This meant I was back in the Reformed family. My parents were proudly sitting in the pew when their daughter affirmed the faith.

The words from the letter to the Romans that were given to me have become my motto: *'May the God of hope fill you with all joy and peace as you trust in Him, so that you may overflow with hope' (Rom 15:13).* After the vicar had read out these words, the dear man was frightened out of his wits.

From the pew where my parents were sitting, somebody shouted out, *'by the power of the Holy Spirit!'* Everybody turned around.

I didn't, for I knew who was saying this - Aunt Jannie from Emmen. I felt like hiding, but she had come specially to see her favourite niece being confirmed. Of course, I thought that was very kind of her but, being a member of the Pentecostal church, she was a stranger in our family. Worst of all was the fact that she was right. The Reformed vicar had put a full stop after the word 'hope', but Aunt Jannie had been reading along with him in her own pocket Bible. There it was, in black and white: 'by the power of the Holy Spirit.' I don't think the vicar had left it out on purpose but, because

I'm of a cheerful nature, he thought these words suited me.

And he was right in thinking that. For even now, when I am rather down, joy and peace always overcome gloom and moodiness. For instance, right now I'm enjoying peace in my own little house, while Dropje, my cat, is purring pleasantly on my lap.

When I think back to that confirmation service, I find it strangely surprising that, as I said 'Yes', my first association was that of working on the mission field. I immediately linked saying 'Yes' to God with the fact that as a Christian you belong to God and you are not your own. I realised that, from then on, He could use me for his Kingdom. I knelt down by my bedside on the Sunday evening after my confirmation and prayed rather precociously, 'Lord, I understand that you have a right to my life. I want to serve you, but don't send me to Africa, for that's not my thing.'

I did like London however. While at secondary school, I had visited London and I decided to go there for a holiday after my first year at Jelburg college. My parents didn't approve, but by now they had come to understand that it was difficult to talk me out of anything. Besides I had decided to stay in the London YWCA and the C of

Homeless men in London.

Christian was in that name. One way or another I felt at home in that metropolis and I loved roaming the streets among people from so many different backgrounds. I also loved being anonymous and just absorbing all the impressions. The one thing I didn't like was the weather, but that too was typically London and I was not inclined to go back home. At the YWCA office I read a small advert seeking volunteers to come and give help to the homeless. *The Simon Community urgently needs volunteers to help the Down-and-Outs of London. Please join us!'* I thought I could just go and have a look. After all, I had not been to the North East of London. I got on the tube, and looked for the Simon Community. I was startled - first of all because of the neighbourhood. If you have never visited that part of London before, you have not missed a thing!

Then there was the house. It looked dilapidated and not like a proper shelter for the homeless. When I arrived, there was only one social worker on duty for the two centres, as well as a second-hand clothing shop. Yet the Simon Community turned out to be well-known all over England. Anton Wallich-Clifford, a probation officer, had started it in the early 1960s. Even the famous singer Paul Simon was a patron of this organisation. The name Simon, however, didn't refer to him, but to Simon of Cyrene, the man who was forced to carry Jesus' cross all the way to Golgotha.

The Simon Community was a Christian organisation, but the only things that the homeless received were a roof over their head, a bed and food. The gospel was not mentioned, no questions were asked, everyone was welcome. Nearly every guest was addicted, sometimes to drugs, but mostly to alcohol.

Soup run with the Simon Community

Without exception they were people who did not count in society, down-and-outs. I decided I would stop enjoying my holiday in the rain and started volunteering.

The YWCA lady was visibly shocked when I collected my suitcase and told her of my plans. 'Far too dangerous for a girl like you,' she commented. Back in the Simon Community I was allocated a bed in the "Birdcage", the room for females. Lots of funny puns were used to alleviate the misery, like using "cadge" (begging) instead of "cage". The shock was immediate and total.

I was dropped in the deep end. That very same evening I went out on the streets with them to hand out food. I found out that it wasn't just the down-and-outs that were poor, the organisation too was penniless.

The food they handed out was the food they went without. Hands in the air, an elderly woman fell to her knees when she was given a piece of bread and a small cup of soup. I could hardly hold back my tears. (Weird to think the English called this type of doughy bread "Mother's Pride".) However, we were a happy bunch and people were very thankful, even though I thought to myself, 'Does this count as a proper meal?'

From somewhere in a pile of junk another homeless friend retrieved a box. He put it in front of him, upside down and solemnly declared, 'My dinner table.' In great style he draped a newspaper over his table and danced around it before he started to eat, a big smile on his face. He had mastered the art of living and knew how to make something out of nothing, even though he looked as if he had made a few mistakes in the past.

My roommate in the Birdcage was a woman who was in a terrible muddle psychologically. Both night and day she walked round in pyjamas, while a reasonable dress was stored in her worn-out little suitcase. She proudly showed it to me. I talked it over with Colin, the other social worker. He told me she had been in pyjamas for weeks on end.

'Please, can I try and change her mind?' I asked him. 'Go ahead', he said calmly. Each time I went to the female wing, I tried to gain the trust of the "pyjama woman". I even gave a kind of fashion show to make her realise that her dress really looked very pretty. After two days I succeeded in getting her to dress normally.

Once she had made that step, she walked around the house as proud as a peacock. We also spent many less innocent moments in the Simon Community. The YWCA lady was right in her warning that the work was dangerous.

I had only been there for a few days when a heavily pregnant woman went completely berserk and attacked me physically.

She was extremely strong. Even if I had been able to take her on, I couldn't have done anything to her because of the baby in her womb. Fortunately some more experienced members of staff were around that day. They quickly ran to where the noise was coming from and, with difficulty, managed to keep the woman in check.

Later that night a new guest arrived. He was agitated and rambling. He was given a bed but he couldn't sleep. Since he was keeping others awake, we sent him to the kitchen. He kept pacing back and forth. When we asked him why he couldn't sleep, he told us he had killed a few people. That was quite scary in a kitchen where knives were accessible. I went and sat on top of the draining board as relaxed as I could, with my legs in front of the cutlery drawer. In the meantime, someone else called the psychiatric hospital where the man might have come from. On inquiry the nurse coolly said that they had released the 'rather aggressive patient' this weekend because of staff shortages.

Of course, coping with the rough circumstances in the Simon Community were far beyond an inexperienced holiday help like me. But the leadership were of a different opinion. That's why they sent a 19-year-old girl to accompany one of the homeless people to the other side of London for him to have a TB examination. It was the first time that I felt something of the humiliation which is the daily experience of homeless people.

A passenger absent-mindedly came and sat beside us. The moment he discovered that my travel companion was a down-and-out, he immediately stood up and, with near audible distaste, walked to the other end of the compartment.

It would be interesting to try out this little experiment in Amsterdam: Let a blob of snot drip down your chin, rub onion soup in your hair, fasten your buttonless coat with a rope for a belt, put on worn-out shoes without laces and enjoy the effects!

I felt especially sorry for the so-called decent, middle-class men and women. Their behaviour was so rude that I wondered which person really was the poor soul. I felt the same anger again that I had felt at primary school when Johanna was being badly bullied by "the strong ones". I snuggled up a bit closer to my travel companion to show him I was not ashamed of him.

I felt more and more that this was the place where I belonged. After a few weeks in the Simon Community, I decided I would come back at the first opportunity which turned out to be during the Christmas break. It was going to be my first-ever birthday away from my family - not so nice for my parents and my brother, but the homeless in London had stolen my heart.

This time I was asked to help in Simonwell Farm in Canterbury, a kind of a Charles Dickens setting for Christmas, especially when there was snow. In reality the atmosphere was a little less romantic. My job was to collect money in Canterbury's many pubs, with the help of a bunch of residents. It was a cross between a

Simonwell Farm

Salvation Army collection and a pub-crawl. Especially around Christmas, collecting money wasn't a big problem. It was more difficult to drag the "collectors" with me to the next pub, without them first tanking themselves up with alcohol. At one place, a particular "collector" went too far and the whole group was thrown out. Inside the houses alcohol was not really prohibited. Of course, it was not a sensible idea, but because a number of staff really found it difficult to handle alcohol, supervision was an impossible task.

The experience of the pub-crawl was followed by another event. A member of staff met me at the entrance and advised me to walk upstairs straight away.

One of the residents had slashed his wrists and was bleeding to death in the men's ward. Soon afterwards I heard an ambulance arrive and the man was taken away in a critical condition. At 4am we received a phone call from the hospital, 'Please come and collect him. He is well enough to come home.' It sounded cynical, as if they were ignorant of the fact that this man was homeless. They also knew that he wanted to die as soon as possible. Was there really no bed available in the hospital? It sounded like a modern version of the nativity story - no room in the inn. In the middle of the night, I was sent out to find a cab in the deserted streets to fetch a suicidal man from hospital.

On Christmas Day I celebrated my twentieth birthday in a home along with twenty homeless men. If only my parents could have seen me sitting halfway up the stairs holding a baseball bat. A drunk heroin addict had objected violently after a homosexual guest of Simonwell Farm wanted to say 'Merry Christmas' by kissing everybody. Like a Speedy Gonzales, the addict chased the poor lad with a large bread knife, meaning to kill him. After our over-friendly guest had run up the stairs past me, the other members of staff managed to overpower the man wielding the knife. Minutes later the phone rang.

It was the leadership of the Simon Community in London wanting to wish us 'Merry Christmas'. I picked up the receiver and said, 'Merry Christmas? What are you talking about?' I wasn't used to the tradition of saying 'Merry Christmas'. I heard laughter at the other end of the line, 'Are you drunk or something, not knowing about Merry Christmas?' 'I am probably the only one who is *not* drunk,' I replied. At that moment everybody cried out in unison, 'Merry Christmas!' What I had told them was not far from the truth.

Christmas in the Simon Community had very little to do with religion and we were hardly aware of all the Christmas fuss happening outside in the shops and streets. For me religion consisted mostly in social concern. My two main motives for doing this work and spending all my free time on it, were my conviction that it was wrong to ignore marginalised people who needed compassion and my anger towards the majority of people who didn't seem to care.

These days my attitude is very different. From my conversations with Dik I concluded that my passion to improve the world made high demands on myself. Aunt Jannie was spot-on when she interrupted that beautiful confirmation service with the Bible phrase that the vicar had omitted: *'by the power of the Holy Spirit.'*

What does that mean? When I was in the Simon Community, I didn't realise that improving the world in your own strength will wear you out. Even after my confirmation this truth didn't really sink in. I was paying the price. I only had to think that I needed to achieve something and I was tired out.

◆ ◆ ◆

I shall take a little break before I continue my story. And Dropje needs some food. He is hanging around me and letting out a plaintive 'meow' from time to time. As soon as I can I will try and continue to share my experiences in England with you. I continued to go there, despite my illness. Obviously, I didn't visit the Simon Community, for that would have been too much for me. But I am happy to tell you about my British adventure which took place after the Simon Community. That experience completely turned my world upside down.

Before I do that, I want to let you read what I wrote in my diary this week:

Wednesday - *Compassion for other people – is that part of my character or is it because I feel such need for protection myself?*

Thursday - Awfully *tired and sad. Why? I don't know. What must I do to break this vicious cycle?*

As you can see, a lot more needed to happen before I could function normally.

Chapter 4

A nice speaker

Sunday - I can hardly imagine what unconditional love looks like. That God would answer my prayer without me having to do something in return. With my mind I know that it works like that, but I hope that someday I will believe it with my heart.

Wednesday - I often have trouble with people who are different and I don't take them the way they are. I really want them to meet all my requirements. This is nonsense, of course. I'll try to pay attention to that.

Saturday - Sometimes I have the feeling that I have to do something special in order to be appreciated, even though right now my friends around me think I'm ok. When will I be good enough in my own eyes?

These are just a few of my diary entries written around eighteen months after I became unwell. I noticed that talking and writing about myself was becoming a little easier. The friends I mentioned were mainly people from the area around Sommelsdijk and Middelharnis, twin councils on Goeree-Overflakkee.
My birthday was a lot of fun. Although I had only been living there for a short time, I came to know quite a few people and some became friends.

How did I come to live here? After graduation I was offered a job in a home for young offenders in Amersfoort. It was demanding work that required my constant, undivided attention.

I hadn't been working there very long when I had to have an operation. For years I had been suffering from an unpleasant condition called endometriosis. It has to do with monthly periods and causes unbearable pain in the abdomen. After the surgery my work in Amersfoort became too taxing physically.

In Middelharnis a vacancy came up for a counsellor in De Proeftuin, a centre for youngsters who have to go to school part-time. These teenagers usually have learning and behavioural difficulties and often leave school early, but they are too young to work full-time. I was taken on and had been working and living there for a few years at this point.

I joined an inter-church Bible Group, which was really good! We didn't talk about our differences but about the essential points in the Bible. Only then do you discover that all Christians have a common foundation, the Bible and the Lord Jesus. The people in the Bible Group became my friends, demonstrated by the love they showed me when I was ill.

But I have promised to share about my contacts in England. Previously I told you that, after I started college, I went and visited the Simon Community whenever I had some days off. One of the volunteers I met there was Alan, a young man about my age who was studying at Seale-Hayne Agricultural College. It turned out that his girlfriend, Yvonne, was Dutch. Yvonne and I hit it off straight away and we became close friends. Back home in Holland we also kept in touch. Alan was going to the south-west of England on a work placement and ended up living in a caravan on a country estate in Devon.

When visiting Alan and Yvonne from then on, I noticed something had changed. They now took their faith very seriously, had given up smoking and, when Alan came to the Netherlands, he didn't sleep at Yvonne's, but stayed elsewhere.

In time, Alan and Yvonne got married and went to live in Devon. During my next holiday period while working at the Simon Community, I phoned Yvonne to arrange to meet up.

Enthusiastically she asked me, 'Will you come and stay with us next weekend?' I rather liked the idea but was a bit taken aback when she added, 'We have such a nice speaker.' That remark made me feel slightly queasy but, because I didn't want to disappoint her, I promised I would spend the weekend with them. I took the train and enjoyed the lovely scenery. It was the first time I realised what a beautiful country England is. The last part of the journey was spent on the coach along narrow, winding, country lanes. From the bus stop where I got off, I still had to walk quite a way. The roads here were so narrow that there was not room for two cars to pass. To the left and right, high hedges obscured the view, except when standing on top of a hill. Then the hedges looked like long ribbons, dividing the scenery into what seemed like life-size pieces of a jigsaw, fresh green with bright yellow patches of gorse.

When I arrived at the entrance of the long driveway, I noticed that, unconsciously, I was holding my breath for a second. What a picture! The large house was painted soft pink and stood out in stunning

Rora House

contrast to the palette of all those shades of green and brown. 'Wow,' I thought, 'this is fantastic! I will go out walking and enjoy the countryside.'

Then I remembered the nice speaker that Yvonne had been telling me about. 'I suppose he could throw a spanner in the works,' I thought to myself. 'Why ever did they think I wanted to come and listen to a nice speaker? They must think that I, being a good, Reformed girl, know everything about the Christian faith.

What on earth has happened to them?'

Alan told me once that his parents were Anglicans and also that he had not set foot in a church since he was fifteen. As far as I know Yvonne didn't go to church at all. Pondering all this, I walked up the driveway.

Fineke and Yvonne, 1979

I heard an enthusiastic 'Welcome to Rora House'. Yvonne grabbed hold of me and greeted me with a big kiss. 'Come on, let's go down to our caravan and after that I'll show you round the main building where you'll be sleeping.' The caravan was beautifully hidden among some of the ancient trees which give the grounds their magnificent character. I again noticed how much Alan and Yvonne had changed. Their use of language was one of those changes. It was mainly in the Simon Community that I learned how to speak English.

Without realising it, I used a lot of swear words. I sensed that here at Rora, it was not appropriate to use words like "shit" and "bloody", though Alan and Yvonne never commented when I slipped up. Neither did they mention the fact that I was smoking like a chimney. I was amazed at the transformation that had taken place in their lives - at their kindness and patience. But there was more to come.

After Yvonne had shown me my bedroom in the beautiful main building, she introduced me to some more people who lived in Rora House. Surprisingly there were a lot of young people my age. There was a happy and positive atmosphere. Yet a few questions puzzled me - like the fact that I had seen two people sitting with their eyes closed and their arms around one another's shoulders.

'Strange,' I thought, 'it looks as if they are praying.'

In general though, everyone was fairly down-to-earth and there was no lack of English humour.

After tea Yvonne asked, 'Well…what are you going to do? Are you coming to the meeting?'

As casually as I could, I said, 'That's right, you mentioned this nice speaker!'

Yvonne laughed. 'You are Reformed, aren't you? You must know then what I mean?' 'No, not really,' I said, hoping Yvonne would tell me some more. I didn't have to wait long.

While walking past a neatly mown lawn, the truth came out.

Yvonne said, 'Recently Alan and I have been converted'.

In my imagination I saw a spectre of sects and asked, 'What do you mean by that?'

'Well, I mean that we have been converted to the Christian faith and from now on Jesus is the Lord of our lives.'

I swallowed hard and said spontaneously, 'Converted? But you already were such nice people. Why did you have to be converted?'

'You not only need conversion when your whole life is a mess, like the people in the Simon Community. Every person needs to be converted. I thought you would know that. Didn't you grow up with the teaching that everyone has sinned? Oh, I'm preaching at you…Just come along tonight. Maybe things will become clearer then.' With a grin I said, 'I don't think so, but ok, I will come.'

That night took a bit of getting used to. I had to admit that the English were good at singing and that was a great intro for me since I simply loved music. Every now and again I looked at Yvonne out of the corner of my eye. She was beaming and sometimes her eyes filled with tears. She was a down-to-earth Dutch girl, so I thought to myself that this must be real.

Nothing at all made it look like a sect. And the nice speaker turned out to be a very normal man, who simply explained the Bible.

He pointed out that believing is a matter of obeying God.

The core of the message was that every person can be used by

God, no matter how intelligent, physically fit or financially sound. 'The only condition is that you hand over control of your life to God. All you have to do is acknowledge Jesus, the Son of God, as Lord.' Strangely enough every word seemed to have more depth and go deeper than I was used to with sermons.

I did find it a little disturbing that people kept on saying 'Amen'.

I thought to myself, 'I wonder if they say this because people here are in the habit of saying it or because they really agree with this man'.

I had to admit that everything made sense. Something in my heart said 'Amen' as well.

When the speaker, whose name was Malcolm, asked whether there was anybody who was not sure that Jesus was Lord of his or her life, I spontaneously raised my hand. I thought to myself, 'I don't have to fuss about that.' If I had realised what the next question was going to be, I might have thought again. 'Will you acknowledge Him as Lord tonight?' There was no going back. In for a penny, in for a pound. So, much louder than I intended, I said, 'Yes!' I was taken aback by this and looked over to Yvonne. She laughed and threw me a kiss, as a big tear ran down her cheek. Not much had changed, except that I began to feel more at home among these enthusiastic believers.

It was late when we finally settled down to sleep.

In the middle of the night, though, I woke up in a panic. My body was covered in sweat. I had had a terrible dream, hideous monsters were dancing around me, pulling my arms and legs. It was as if I was hanging between heaven and earth and they intended to smash me up. At that moment I woke up. It had been so real that I pulled the blankets over myself for fear of the monsters. It was not until dawn that a sense of safety returned.

Over breakfast I didn't mention this to Yvonne. Strangely enough, however, the sermon that morning was about the invisible world, a subject I had never heard anything about.

According to the speaker, a battle is taking place between angels and demons. In this battle mankind is at stake and in particular man's mind and thoughts.

This reminded me of my dream. 'Were those monsters real after all?' The speaker said, 'The battle increases when a person acknowledges Jesus as Lord of his life. At that moment the evil powers know they are losing territory.'

I thought to myself, 'What is this? Do these people know what I went through last night?' After the meeting I told the speaker everything.

The man was not surprised and thought it quite normal. He said, 'Jesus is your secret weapon. He is your Lord and He is the one who is pulling the strings. All power belongs to Him ever since He was raised from the dead. If ever you are harassed again, just confess that aloud.' The next night I slept like a baby.

The weekend I spent at Rora House turned my life upside down. It felt a bit strange going back to the Simon Community. However, it was not at odds with what I had just experienced. For the first time I realised that not only the destitute are in need of help. A well brought up, Reformed young lady is just as much in need of help. For the time being I kept silent about the weekend at Rora House. People from the street see right through wonderful tales. They see very clearly whether you live what you preach. But the proof of the pudding is in the eating.

Back in the Netherlands I had a wonderful internship at the Hoogeland Stichting in Beekbergen, a reception centre for socially vulnerable men, many of whom were homeless. I worked with over eighty men and was the first woman to be employed, because of the experience I had gained in London. It was a taxing job, but very rewarding. During my holidays, I almost always returned to Rora House, considering it my spiritual home.

As I said before, my abdominal pains were increasing. Soon after graduation I had to undergo an operation.

I also found out that my blood type is Rhesus negative, so having children might not be a realistic expectation. I was still young, but even so I started to wonder what my life would be like without children or maybe even without a husband.

After having spent yet another week in England, I was in the car on the way home and was seriously thinking about my future. I had started to grow fond of a young man I had met at Rora and was asking God for clarity on a possible future relationship.

'What if I want you to stay single?'
It sounded as if somebody was sitting beside me in the car. I was shocked - even more so by the thought of remaining single. I went for miles and miles without being able to answer the question. In the end I said, 'All right, Lord, if you want me to. But then I trust I will not have to feel lonely.' At that moment I felt very calm and happy; I was sure that God would go before me.

When I started in De Proeftuin, things were going quite well. However, it is a school and not a care institution. I had grown used to working in a close-knit team. I had also learned to intervene quickly when a situation seemed to be getting out of hand.

At De Proeftuin I came across a very different culture. Everything seemed to revolve around position and results. I realised I couldn't handle that very well. I saw things that needed improvement, but according to the rules they were beyond my responsibility. The management were irritated when I expressed my opinion. They thought I should just carry on with my work, without worrying about other matters.

I couldn't do that however, or rather, I didn't want to.

During the talks I had with Dik, it become clear to me that De Proeftuin was not the only cause of my sickness. It was all so complicated. I read somewhere that endometriosis can cause nervous exhaustion because it upsets the hormone balance.

My doctor, however, said that was nonsense, but he considered a lot of things to be nonsense. He was not at all helpful.

I had already applied for a few other jobs, but it all came to nothing. Who would want somebody who was stressed out?

The management of De Proeftuin hoped that I will be declared unfit for work, so they could get rid of me legally.

Happily, the relationship with my colleagues was still good. To keep up the contact I paid brief visits every now and again. But the management even took that the wrong way and perceived it as stirring things up. I thought that was mean as I only went there to keep in touch with my colleagues. They were really nice and enquired sympathetically as to when I would be back.

The management tried to arrange a physical examination with my medical doctor. I thought, 'Let them get on with it! I am not afraid, because God cares for me.' I realised more and more that God loved me the way I was and He did not continually require me to achieve things. That thought gave me faith for the future. Why then should I complain?

This is what I wrote in my diary:
It is pride to think about yourself in a different way than God does. And God abhors pride. I have to learn to take myself as I am. I am not so dreadfully tired anymore; now and again I do feel listless though.

The next morning I wrote:
I would like a job where I receive appreciation, where I am needed. And I want to work with people, of course, if possible in a Christian organisation.

Chapter 5

Baptised three times over

The world looks so different after recovering from illness. I could enjoy things so much better. Sometimes I walked for miles along the beach or went to the mud flats, a nature reserve close by. Sometimes you could even see common cranes or spoonbills that literally spooned up their food with their big flat beaks. Of course, now that autumn had arrived, they had left for warmer regions. I would have gladly joined them for it was getting quite chilly.

More importantly, the dark clouds that had occupied my mind for so long had largely disappeared. From time to time a depression still descended, like the time when I applied for a job with a national Christian organisation. (Perhaps I was too eager, because I even sent the director a birthday card. Admittedly, that was not appropriate.) However, it did hurt a little when, after a seemingly endlessly wait, I received a letter saying they didn't employ people who had a history of mental health problems. As if that was not enough, they added that they only worked with "mentally mature people". The person who thought that up must have been very self-assured. Who on earth feels "mentally mature"? I don't, that's for sure. I must take care that I don't brand such an organisation as anti-social or even unchristian.

In fact, it was easier to understand that De Proeftuin wanted to get rid of me. They had known me when I was at my worst, but the results of the psychological evaluation were different from what the management had expected. The psychiatrist was of the opinion that many things from my past had not been properly dealt with. He concluded that I had needed a two year 'time-out' to put things right and come to myself.

Therefore I was declared fit for work and De Proeftuin was obliged to re-employ me. Egbert, one of my colleagues, was kind enough to create a new job for me, and so then I began coaching girls who were preparing to start a training course in Health Care. I quite liked it. I could see so much of myself in those girls. Some of them had never received a compliment, either in school, or at home. So, it is no wonder they gave up. They had started to play truant from school and, in the end, they were expelled. I hoped I could motivate them to do something positive with their lives.

Yet I sensed that I would not be at De Proeftuin for very long. Changes were ahead. Maybe you will remember one entry in my diary, when I wrote that I had the feeling of being at a crossroads. As my health recovered, that feeling became clearer.

When I was at Rora last summer, I dared to tell those gathered about my life. Maybe the most difficult thing was to tell them about the moment when God asked me, 'What would you think if you were to remain single and would therefore never marry?'

Shortly afterwards I read a passage in my Bible which greatly encouraged me: 'Sing, o barren woman, you who never bore a child; burst into song, shout for joy, you who were never in labour; because more are the children of the desolate woman than of her who has a husband, says the Lord' (Isaiah 54:1).

Perhaps you will find this hard to understand and so be able to empathise with me, but these words really caused me to shout for joy, even the thought of remaining single and never having children of my own. That is what I told all these people and it made some of them so happy. It seemed that my own inward struggle was somehow meant to encourage other people. Could that possibly be the aim of a church service?

I was also baptised at Rora House and how! Those who come to Christ are baptised by immersion. I can almost hear you say, 'You are going too far now.' Do you know what they do? If they read something in the Bible, they investigate it and then put it into practice. If it turns out that certain things have gone awry over the course of time, they draw their conclusions.

Conference at the grounds of Rora House

In The Netherlands we are not always so receptive, at least not in the church where I grew up. Either you toe the church line or you leave. It seems that doing what it says in the Bible is just too difficult - as if you could catch something from it. I noticed that I felt much better mentally when I did what I felt was right.

Because the Bible says some clear things about baptism, I wanted to follow in obedience. Back home my parents were not enthusiastic about the idea. They were afraid I would become too much like Aunt Jannie. This constant comparison wore me out, but happily I could calmly explain to my parents why I had been baptised for a second time. I told them that I was thankful they had me christened when I was a baby and acknowledged they had very good reasons for doing that. I added, 'That was your faith. Now I have been baptised because of the faith that I have.' Then they accepted it and gave me their support. So my advice is, 'Don't hesitate when God asks you to do something, just be obedient.'

There were other changes during those few months. One of the things I learned at Rora House was that God wants us to go and tell the good news about Jesus to people who have not yet heard it. The people at Rora didn't just talk about it, they themselves were good examples. The work in England was and still is partly led by missionaries and ex-missionaries. You can regularly listen to travel accounts and information from far away countries. As you can imagine, I found this a real blessing.

I thought all these things were only typically English, but on Ascension Day I went to a special event in Amsterdam where a missionary day was organised by the Evangelical Movement in the Netherlands. How come that I had never heard about this before? Thousands of people gathered because they all shared a passion for mission. I was deeply impressed. The atmosphere was similar to that at Rora. The information given was very clear; it looked like a present-day job market. I am fully convinced that mission is the most natural thing in the world. We should all ask ourselves the question whether it is right to stay at home, unless we have been specifically called to do so.

Gradually I was discovering that many Christians in Holland openly professed their faith. Beforehand I had never been aware of this, and I hadn't found it in my church.

This was how I became involved in children's work. My long summer holidays at De Proeftuin allowed me to go and help at the Christian children's camps in Soest. I couldn't believe my eyes and sometimes felt like a child myself. These children heard about God and the Bible in a way that I only first heard at Rora when I was over twenty! With hindsight I was sorry that I hadn't known sooner. It was so lovely to see how children handle the things of God - so real and spontaneous. In Soest I started to reflect on a number of things that were not right in my own life.

I became aware that during every short break I had to go for a walk to satisfy my craving for nicotine. I was like a semi-addict. If I didn't, my need for a cigarette became so strong that I could hardly bear it. Nobody ever told me I should stop, although I had noticed, of course, that Yvonne wasn't smoking any more after she came to the Lord. During this children's camp however, it suddenly became my problem.

I asked a fellow worker if she felt like going for a walk with me. During that walk I told her about my problem. She simply asked me, 'Do you want to quit?'

I said, 'Yes, of course I do. Do you think it's normal to have to sneak out time and again to have a smoke?'

She said casually, 'I can always pray with you.'

I hadn't expected it to be so simple. 'A packet a day is not to be sneezed at,' I said. She happily went on, 'Shall we pray here then?'

We knelt down on a sandy lane, not far from the children's camp. She laid her hands on my head and prayed that I would be freed from smoking. At that moment I realised the stupidity of my addiction and I confessed it to God. I don't know how He did it, but after this simple little prayer I didn't feel like smoking anymore. I have never touched a cigarette since. It was a real miracle. Apparently, God thought it very important that I didn't smoke any more, otherwise He wouldn't have answered that simple prayer so amazingly quickly.

Something else happened during this same children's camp. As I told you before, while in England I learned to take the Bible seriously. It is written about Jesus that He came to baptise people in the Holy Spirit. John the Baptist had said: '*I baptise you with water for repentance. But after me will come one who is more powerful than I, whose sandals I am not fit to carry. He will baptise you with the Holy Spirit and with fire*' (Matt. 3:11).

Many Christians are of the opinion that you receive the Holy Spirit at the moment that you are baptised.

In a sense that is correct, for without the Holy Spirit it is impossible to repent of your sins and be converted.

But 'baptising' is more than 'receiving'. When you baptise something in water it will get wet right through.

Baptism is the same as immersion.

When you are baptised in the Holy Spirit, you are being immersed in the Spirit of God, as it were. This baptism is just as necessary as the baptism in water. This experience is so overwhelming and you never ever forget it. Please, don't get me wrong. This doesn't guarantee that from now on you make no more mistakes. I wish it was like that. God doesn't force anybody to live a holy life. Every day you have to choose whether or not you want to cooperate with God. But He does want to help you. The baptism in the Holy Spirit helps you overcome reluctance to embrace a holy way of life. From that moment on you know how much power and energy He can give you in order to do the will of God, even when everything goes wrong.

The Holy Spirit gives you the desire to do God's will. In the Psalms you read about Jesus: *'I desire to do your will, O my God; your law is within my heart' (Psalm 40:8)*. The same can be said about the followers of Jesus.

I went to the children's camp to be a leader, but discovered that I also had to become like a child. To be honest, I have to admit that I had remained a kind of tough girl who thought she was in control of most things, but on that particular Wednesday I had to surrender my pride and confess that I was addicted to smoking. Maybe that also broke my resistance to the work of the Holy Spirit.

After the leaders of the children's work prayed for me, I was overwhelmed and completely lost control. What joy I had! I have no idea how long I was thanking and praising God in a language I didn't understand. In England I had heard about speaking in tongues but when it was given to me it was completely different from what I expected - not at all difficult or complicated. I just opened my mouth and then these words I had never learned and did not understand flowed out. Deep down in my heart though I knew that I was talking to God. This was my third baptism.

It is a wonderful experience that I would wish for anybody. Look it up in your Bible and, if you also desire this baptism, ask God. He will never leave you out in the cold. He doesn't give you a snake instead of a fish (*Luke 11:13*).

In England they had told me there was a small church in Klaaswaal where people also believed all these things that were so new to me. This church was not far from where I lived.

Like in England, mission was often talked about in Klaaswaal. One of the leaders, Piet Punt, even ended up leaving his well-paid job to go to South America with his wife Marijke and their children.

After the Christian organisation had sent me the awkward letter saying they couldn't use me because I had had a breakdown, I had given up the idea of going into missions myself, yet I could not ignore or forget Piet and Marijke's stories. I didn't discuss this with anybody for fear of being disappointed again.

For the first time I saw at close quarters how God was speaking to people about their future. Piet and Marijke had been convinced for quite some time that they would go to the mission field, but they had no idea about which country. As a family they meditated and prayed about this. After some time, in a dream Marijke saw the whole map of South America. She recognised several countries like Venezuela and Chile, but in the dream she very clearly heard a voice saying, 'I want you to go to Bolivia.' Bolivia – that country had never crossed her mind. She had never even read anything about it.

The following day Marijke said to Piet, 'I had a very strange dream. I think I know the name of the country where we should go'. 'Hush,' Piet said, 'Don't tell me. I believe God will also reveal it in another way. If the two agree, we will know that it has God's approval. So, why don't you write it down and hide it in a place that's only known to you.'

A year later, twelve-year-old Annemiek asked her mother, 'Mum, how does God speak? Can He speak through a thought that keeps coming back?' Marijke said: 'Why do you ask that?'

'Well, maybe you'll think it's silly,' the girl answered, 'but for about a year now I keep thinking of Bolivia.'

Marijke could hardly believe her ears. Without letting Annemiek in on her amazement, she first went to her husband and told him what she had just heard. Piet did think it strange that God would give a clear indication on the future of the whole family to his wife and daughter and not to him, but he too found himself at peace about going to Bolivia.

Two years later the whole family left for La Paz.
The Punt family had been in Bolivia for a few months and from what I heard they were doing well. Their plans had to change a great deal though. I wondered how they had managed through that time. You may realise that I had become very curious. That's why I decided to spend my holidays with Piet and Marijke in Bolivia.

Chapter 6

Close to the sun

My connections with Bolivia actually started while I was still at school. It's strange, isn't it? I had been in Bolivia for a couple of weeks when I suddenly remembered that I had once written an essay on this country while I was at secondary school. Some facts about Bolivia seemed strangely familiar to me.

The city of La Paz

For example the country is nearly 27 times the size of The Netherlands, and was named after Simon Bolivar, who lived during the reign of Napoleon.

This was also the man who liberated South America from Spanish rule. I also remembered that La Paz is a city situated at one of the highest altitudes in the world. I found that out at my cost! I was very sick and had a violent headache. On my arrival the Punt family was very kind to me. For the first few days I didn't have to do anything. Indeed, I wouldn't have been able to.

Just taking ten steps was comparable to climbing the Dom Tower in Utrecht. In addition, Piet and Marijke were living in a small, very steep street. Every other minute I had to stand still to get my breath back and my heart was racing. It became easier over time as my body gradually acclimatised.

La Paz and El Alto together form one large city with around one and a half million inhabitants. El Alto is the new upper city at 4,200 metres above sea level. The airport is here, and is the highest international airport in the world. La Paz is the old city lower down in the valley which is shaped like a horseshoe. I was already breathless as I entered the arrival lounge of the airport with my cabin luggage. Piet and Marijke were waiting for me. The trip to the centre of La Paz took about an hour. It was the nicest part of a long journey which, all in all, had lasted more than 24 hours, waiting times included. I couldn't believe my eyes.

Firstly, there was the breath-taking panorama of the city centre, deep down in the valley. The houses, slums and other buildings were built against the steep slopes in a higgledy-piggledy way. But the rugged mountain tops of the Andes impressed me most – as I was a girl from the low countries. The highest peak is Illimani at a height of almost 6,500 metres. The snow-capped top was shining in the bright sunshine, standing out in sharp relief against a clear, blue sky.

Once we were down in the city centre the traffic chaos was incredible. We could only edge forward bit by bit, which I didn't mind at all. This way I had the opportunity to absorb the impressions of this wondrous world of South American Indian people, white people and everybody in between.

I was particularly taken by those beautiful small Indian people with their wonderfully golden complexions. The women had long, raven, braided hair with English bowler hats jauntily perched on top of their heads. The men had straight hair, cut squarely above their dark, bright eyes and sharp features.

Almost all the indigenous women were wearing brightly coloured shawls in which they carried all manner of things. Their wide skirts reached almost down to the ground and gave the impression that being fat was the norm.

(At least I wouldn't have to worry so much about my figure.)

We were queuing amidst jam-packed taxi vans. Hanging out of the rear window of each van, a co-driver announced the stops at an incredible speed. I couldn't understand a word and wondered if I would ever be able to learn this language.

From the car it looked like a lovely summer day, but no one seemed to be enjoying the sunshine. Marijke told me it's best not to sit out in the sun, because the ozone layer in this part of the world is dangerously thin - hence all the hats, shawls and people seeking the shade. It's a pity for us Dutch who want to catch every ray of sunshine. I hadn't realised that during our summer months it is the middle of winter in Bolivia. Because of the high altitude one doesn't realise that one is close to the Equator. Especially on the high plains, the cold in winter is fierce.

Even when I was indoors I wore several layers of clothing, for the houses lacked sufficient heating. In the lower city, the temperature will rise to around 20 degrees at 3pm. As soon as the sun disappears behind the horizon though, the temperature falls to zero. It was striking to see how many people were out on the streets when it was so bitterly cold.

Even late at night the streets were filled with market stalls where men and women, warmly wrapped up like mummies, were patiently waiting for customers. I also noticed the beggars, the homeless and countless boys and girls trying to earn some money doing odd jobs. I wondered how many of them spent all night out on the street, and I was troubled at all the overt drunkenness. It seemed similar to North East London. Would there be a kind of Simon Community here?

Of course, I could not see all of the country in the few weeks I was there. Bolivia is as large as Spain and France put together. No other comparison will hold. In the west, where I was, the snow-capped mountain tops and bare, vast plains dominate the landscape, but towards the east Bolivia becomes more friendly. There the Andes mountains change into subtropical Yungas and tropical lowlands, towards the border with Brazil. The cultural roots of the Bolivians are not to be found in the tropical part, but in the Andes, on the high plains and especially around *Lake Titicaca.*

With the Punt family I visited Titicaca, the highest navigable lake in the world and the cradle of the Indian culture. Long before the name Bolivia was used, even before the Inca rule, Aymara
were living there. They are the Indian tribe that even now forms the majority in this part of the country. At one time South America was a patchwork of Indian tribes. Each had their own gods, their own language and culture. Yet everyone agrees that the spiritual

centre of all Indians was somewhere near Lake Titicaca, with the sacred town of Tiwanaku. In Aymara language this is "Taypi Qala", which means "stone in the centre".
The Tiwanaku temple
was devoted to Tunupa, the god of all natural elements.

Today only a ruin remains, but Tupuna's image can still be seen on the "Puerta del Sol", Spanish for "gate of the sun". I visited all these sites, but they gave me an eerie feeling. This unease increased when I met Dutch tourists travelling from Tibet to Tiwanaku as New Age pilgrims to restore ancient pre-Christian rituals. When the sun reaches a certain position, they swarm to these places. For good reason Bolivia is called the "Tibet of the Americas".

= *Aymara territory*

It is the spiritual centre of all Indian tribes, from Colombia to Argentina and maybe even from Alaska to Tierra del Fuego.

The Aymara culture reached its peak in Tiwanaku. However, in the 14th century another Indian tribe rose to power, the Quechuas, better known as the Incas. They were taller, with a lighter complexion and surpassed the Aymaras militarily and economically.

According to some historians, the conquest happened peacefully, but others claim that massacres took place. In any case there was discrimination. The Quechuas felt superior to the Aymaras, but they respected their language, customs and religion. Aymaras and Incas believe in good and evil spirits that inhabit material things. Spirits even live in pots and pans in the kitchen. "Isla del Sol", "Island of the Sun", is situated in the middle of Lake Titicaca, not far from Tiwanaku. The Incas regarded the sun as the supreme god and called him "Inti". The king of the Quechuas was a god as well, and his summer residence was also to be found on the Isla del Sol.

High up in the Andes Mountain range, Pachacuti later built the famous town of Cusco boasting a much larger sun temple than the old Tiwanaku.
Cusco became the capital of the vast Inca empire.

Pachacuti the Inca made a surprising discovery which most researchers and New Age followers would like to suppress. While being a devoted Inti worshipper, Pachacuti was literally overshadowed by an alarming thought, 'How is it possible that the most high god can be obscured by a simple cloud? How can something that

Cusco

has been created affect the creator?' Slowly it was dawning on the king that the sun could not possibly be the almighty God. That also meant that all those magnificent buildings, covered with gold, built in honour of Inti, had been built in vain. The llama and human sacrifices made in honour of Inti had all just been the work of man. There had to be a Creator, exalted high above the sun.

Pachacuti remembered that at one time his father Hatun Tupac had been given a revelation in a dream. It was about a God who had introduced himself as the Creator of heaven and earth. This God was called 'Viracocha'. However, Hatun Tupac had not pursued this dream.

Pachacuti decided that the Creator of heaven and earth had to be honoured and called together the Council of Wise Men. He said what he believed and pointed out his threefold doubt about the deity of the sun god Inti:

1. Inti cannot be a universal god if he shines on one man while another man is in darkness.
2. He cannot be perfect because he never rests and always moves at the same speed.
3. He cannot be almighty for even the smallest of clouds can block out his light.

But who was Viracocha according to King Pachacuti?

These are the words that have been attributed to him:

'Viracocha is eternal, at a distance, exalted and uncreated. By his word he created all men, as well as all spirits. He is the happiness of all people, he gives the gift of life through his created son, Punchao (the sun disc). He is the bringer of peace and order. He is the blessed one and has compassion on fallen man. He only judges them and gives mercy and enables them to overcome their anger.'

A shock wave went through the gathering of Wise Men. This new teaching would turn the whole of the Inca culture upside down. The idea that Inti would no longer receive the highest honour was so revolutionary that it was decided not to include the common people.

Only the royal family was to observe the worship of the Creator of heaven and earth.

King Pachacuti died but the expectation lived on that the Son of the Creator was coming. (*Source: 'Eternity in their hearts' – Don Richardson 1984)*

When the first white people set foot ashore and reached Cusco on horseback, King Atawalpa, the successor of Pachacuti, thought that the leader Pizarro was the long-awaited Son of God. Pizarro was a cunning merchant and had noted all the gold and riches of the temples. He asserted that he indeed was the long-awaited redeemer, proceeded to capture Atawalpa and then killed him. What a peacemaker he was!

Pizarro and his men craftily made use of the fact that not everybody was happy with Inca rule. There was a lot of dissatisfaction among the Aymara and other Indian tribes. In this way he managed to undermine Inca dominion. When more troops came over from Spain and Portugal, the conquest of South America became a reality. The 'conquistadores' from Spain wreaked such havoc that trust in white Christians was irreparably damaged.

The Indian people have suffered more than any other people in the world. Justifiably we are deeply shocked by the murder of six million Jews by the Nazis. In South America and especially on the plains of the Andes ten times more Indians were sent to their deaths. Slaves from Africa were in a better position than the original inhabitants of South America. Black people received wages but Indians were even lower than slaves, totally at the disposal of any European. Tens of thousands were deployed down in the silver mines, never to come out alive.

At infant school we learned this song: *'Piet Hein, small is his name but great are his deeds, he has conquered the silver fleet'.* That treasure fleet and the colonisation by the Europeans cost the lives of between sixty and eighty million Indians, not only by slavery and genocide, but also by epidemics of smallpox, measles and influenza against which the Indians had no resistance. *(Source: David Stannard in 'American Holocaust: Columbus and the conquest of the New World', 1992)*

What is left of the high expectation of Pachacuti? Modern day Indians still hope for the God who will come to save. Sadly, they are returning to ancient traditional folk religions. Encouraged by Western anthropologists and the New Age movement, there is a turning back to the worship of the sun and Mother Nature. Thankfully, people are also coming to Jesus and the Christian church is growing.

If, five hundred years ago, the Inca had heard the Biblical message of the gospel, massive numbers would probably have come to faith. But the Quechua, Aymara and the many other Indian tribes of South America have become embittered and are still outraged at five hundred years of exploitation and murder, in fact some exploitation still exists. What was the Catholic church doing throughout these centuries? Didn't they point the people to Jesus?

Although there have been some good influences, in general the Catholic church has mingled with the old Indian pantheism.

The common people, for instance, associate the altar in the Catholic church with an animistic table of sacrifice.

They have changed the word 'mass' into 'mesa' (table) and that makes a big difference. The Latin word "missa" is derived from the final words at the last supper: "Ite, missa est". That means: "Go, be sent forth".
But to many Indians the table of sacrifice is the place where sacrifices are made to idols. Over the last ten years the practice of sacrificing animals to the gods has greatly increased. On the hills and mountains just as many sacrifices are made these days as during the ancient Inca rule.

materials for the sacrifices

Usually, white llamas or llama foetuses are sacrificed, but sometimes it even includes human sacrifices.
Recently, there have been several instances of someone, often a homeless person, mysteriously disappearing. Rumour has it that they were buried in the foundation of buildings or bridges to ward off evil spirits.

The history of the Indians can make me angry, especially at my own European origin, but the strange thing is that when you talk with converted Christian Indians, they don't show any such anger. I had attended a few Christian meetings with Piet and Marijke and I was beginning to love the Bolivian people more and more. They made eye contact, revealed their personality and at the same time were very modest. I had the impression they were really interested in me. In Bolivia people were much less reserved than in The Netherlands. They were not everybody's friend, but if you offered your friendship and remained loyal, then you could count on theirs.

I noticed that Piet and Marijke's children felt at ease, which to me said a lot. Children sense so much better whether people are trustworthy.

Of course I was not in Bolivia as a tourist but sometimes I felt I was prying. My aim was to see how a couple in their forties, the mother and father of three children, managed to make a new life in a strange country, with a language in which they were not fluent and without a specific missionary assignment. In such a situation it is of great importance to know that you have been sent by the Father. Initially they had come to plant a new church in La Paz, but that had fallen through. So they were travelling  *Piet and Marijke Punt.* around remote areas giving Bible studies on behalf of the Bolivian Asambleas de Dios. This was a unique opportunity and maybe it was the work to which the Lord had called them.

However, sometimes one could read the doubt on their faces. Piet is an organiser and technician, Marijke a devoted mother with experience in children's ministry.

They were doing what their hands found to do, enthusiastically and without complaint.

Because I didn't speak Spanish, I was not much use to them. I had my own reasons for being there. Thankfully they did not try to persuade me to move as well. Enthusiasm alone won't get you very far.

Many missionaries have been in Bolivia but couldn't stay the course, not only because of the difficult living conditions, but also because of things that cannot be observed with the naked eye. Christians who have lived here for a very long time have told me it has to do with the spiritual world, with the influence of the occult that dominates the culture of the Indians. Yet I was drawn to this life, not because of an emotional hype or a pipe dream. It's hard to describe what I felt. I knew that if it was up to me, I would like to stay.

Chapter 7

Stopover in Salamanca

Time had flown by and a year had passed since I had visited Bolivia. In autumn 1988 I was living in Salamanca, an old fortified town, three hundred kilometres from Madrid. I came here to learn Spanish and experts say this is the best place to do so. Salamanca is one of the oldest university towns in Spain, a proud city with beautiful cathedrals, theatres and, of course, the monumental university building. The street scene was dominated by trendy, young people, walking from one college to the next, sometimes debating fiercely, piles of thick books under their arms. They took their studies really seriously. In the evenings Salamanca was like a fairy tale. It was as if the illuminated house fronts wanted to hold on to the fading sunlight. The town centre, with its beautiful squares and age-old alleyways was buzzing with happy people, dressed beautifully and engaged in lively conversation. For young and old alike strolling on sultry evenings was the favourite pastime.

Amidst these delicately built Spaniards I felt very Dutch, partly because I am not a nightlife person. Of course my budget played a role in this as well. I still had some money in my Dutch bank account, but for some unknown reason I was unable to access it. So there I was, awaiting an envelope from the home front. Every now and again I ordered some plain rice at the Chinese takeaway. I could see them thinking, is she on a diet? I didn't mind. It would not hurt me to lose a few pounds. Thankfully, I could still pay for the rent on my room. I lived with a Spanish family who were members of an evangelical church in Salamanca. They were nice people, but it was tiring to always be obliged to speak Spanish. At first I wanted to try out every newly learned word, but after a while I got stuck and I wanted to say more than I could. My Spanish course was going well. Time and again I found there was a hump I had to get over and it felt as if my brain couldn't take any more. This "language ceiling" was rather frustrating. Arriving at an impasse is a common experience for language students. Over the past few months I had been crying a lot in my little room, because my brain wouldn't work as fast as I wanted. The few Japanese in my class were the leaders by far. They seemed to learn Spanish very quickly, but I think all they did was to learn the words by heart.

I mixed with Spanish people as much as I could because it was good to practise my Spanish, but also for my personal development. I needed to socialise with people and especially with Christians. That's why I was actively involved in the church. I even went evangelising out on the streets with them. It was a good way to get to know the people better. I discovered that all non-Catholics were labelled sectarians, not only because the Catholic church was so powerful, but also because Jehovah's Witnesses were very active in Spain. It was unpleasant always to be compared with them. But it kept me humble and it made me respect the Spaniards who were honest about their faith and the missionaries who had been working here for decades, despite meagre results.

One group in Spain was an exception in this respect, that was the gypsies. There were dozens of evangelical gypsy churches, one of which was in Salamanca. I went there and what an experience that was. They had songs in their own language and the meetings were very lively, as you might expect of gypsies. When praying, they assumed that God was deaf! They were amazingly warm-hearted, but for the sake of progress in my Spanish I thought it better to join my landlord's church.

Why was I learning Spanish? It is the language spoken in Bolivia. My plans to go to Bolivia were now very serious. In fact, ever since I had returned from Bolivia, I couldn't help thinking about the country. On my way back from Bolivia to The Netherlands something happened which I can't really explain. After an eighteen-hour flight I arrived in Frankfurt. In one way it started there. I kept having a lump in my throat and I thought it was because I was tired. But on the plane to Amsterdam I got worse. Entering the arrivals lounge at Schiphol, I was met by Gert Jan, my pastor from the church in Klaaswaal. When I went over to greet him, I couldn't control myself any longer and started to cry uncontrollably. Gert Jan must have thought that my trip had been a nightmare or that I had narrowly escaped an air disaster.

'What happened to you?' he asked anxiously. I sobbed, 'I have left a piece of my heart behind in Bolivia.' On our way home, Gert Jan listened quietly as I explained to him that in those few weeks a deep love had grown within me for the Bolivian people. 'They are such captivating people. I just love them. I don't know what it is, but the further away I got, the more I started to miss them. I think this is not just being emotional, but I believe God has put this love in my heart.'
Gert Jan then responded, 'If you want to go to Bolivia, I am right behind you, Fineke. If you are still as sure in a couple of weeks' time, you should start making definite plans.
If you don't do anything and just wait, you will never find out whether God wants you to go there or not. And remember, if it turns out it wasn't a good choice after all, I am still behind you. In that case you will have gained experience, and you will still be very welcome in church.'

I had not expected such a great reaction. So I wasn't expected to behave like "the ideal missionary" who is valued as long as she stays abroad. I had already heard about missionaries having to return to The Netherlands because of illness or other setbacks, who had become deeply unhappy because their church didn't know they existed. A few weeks later, my desire to go to Bolivia was still as strong. My work was going fine. I was enjoying my new position at De Proeftuin, yet I knew I wouldn't be working there for much longer.

I shared my plans increasingly openly with my friends and the strange thing was that no one was really surprised. They usually responded by saying, 'Yes, we thought so.'

It was a busy time. On Saturdays, I first attended a course on the tropics in Utrecht and then a course on children's work in Soest.

I thought it was time to inform my work about my plans. But would that be sensible? After all, there was ample time before the compulsory deadline for giving notice. I talked it over with my pastor. He thought it was best to follow my heart in this, rather than taking the official line. Actually handing in my notice was a very emotional moment. There was no turning back and I felt that only now things were really starting to move. The nice thing at work was that my early resignation was appreciated. For me, the importance of that move lay in learning to trust God's voice in my heart.

It was my intention to go to England for the Easter conference. Through Alan and Yvonne, the leadership of Rora House had been informed of my plans. I was asked to say something and had prepared a short slide presentation.

However, on the evening that I was going to share, something happened which was beyond my wildest dreams. Looking back, I think this wouldn't have happened if I had not definitely given up my job with its guarantee of a steady income.

I still wasn't aware of anything when Uncle Joe, one of the leaders at Rora, started to tell a story about a woman who had changed a great deal. 'You wouldn't recognize her now, if you first met her a few years ago,' he said. 'And I want you to promise tonight that you will pray for her in the future, for this woman is about to take up a new responsibility for which she will definitely need your support.'

I really did not know who Uncle Joe was talking about, until he looked in my direction and said, 'Now I would like to ask this woman to come forward, for she has something to say to us.' That gave me a fright. Never had I expected such an introduction.

I was so touched by all those beautiful words that I can't remember anything I said about Bolivia and my mission plans. I do remember though that almost everyone present promised to pray for me. They didn't just say that to be nice, for I knew that they meant it. They weren't only English, but there were also guests from Ireland and even somebody from Australia. That evening I gathered a worldwide support network in one go. These are things only God can do. No publicity campaign could equal this.

The warm response in England made me feel freer about sharing my plans in The Netherlands. During the many Evangelical Alliance Mission days I had attended over the previous years, I had watched how time and again missionaries were prayed for when they were about to leave.

I was a bit scared but phoned the director anyway and told him I was going to language classes to prepare for a missionary assignment in Bolivia. It actually went very smoothly. He had already heard about me and said it was no problem at all to pray for me during the Mission Day.

I was so pleased. I was well aware that I would need a lot of prayer support if I was going to Bolivia for the sake of God's Kingdom.

It is strange, but I notice God is in everything I do. In Spain, as a language student in 1988, I also daily experienced His love and

care. It was not easy by any means. Language study is just sheer hard work and exposes one's limitations. It is also taxing financially and physically. Shall I elaborate? After my second exam, which I passed with flying colours, I developed an inflammation in my left hand, my writing hand. That was a real blow. It was a short course anyway and because of the inflammation I missed a number of weeks. Then I wondered whether I was doing the right thing, whether this was God
telling me to stop. I stayed, probably only because I did not have the money to travel back to The Netherlands. After my hand had healed, I was informed that I was not allowed to make up for missed lessons unless I agreed to register for a further course.

I didn't want to stay in Spain any longer than necessary and I could not afford the expenses. The only alternative was for me to catch up with my own class, which had now moved up a level. I thought that would be an impossible task, but I did it! I caught up reasonably quickly, gaining information on the missed lessons from books. After a month I passed with good marks. I could boast about my flair for languages and the fact I learn easily, but I would not have succeeded without help from my Heavenly Father. Besides, the flair for languages comes from Him, too. With regard to languages, I had had another idea for when I arrived in Bolivia, I wanted to study Aymara, the language spoken by the indigenous people on the plateau. I had noticed that to them Spanish was still the language of the oppressor. Their deepest feelings are best expressed in their own language. I would have to see what happened. It would also have to be God's plan, otherwise I wouldn't do it. There was still so much to do before I actually got to Bolivia.

What strikes me is that many people make a fuss about knowing the will of God. I am not saying that is always easy, but in recent years I have discovered that doing the will of God gives a lot of joy. Even during the time that I was off sick at home, I noticed time and again that He was involved in it and that I mostly needed to learn patience.

In the Bible I read: "*Whether you turn to the right or to the left, your ears will hear a voice behind you, saying, 'This is the way: walk in it'" (Isaiah 30: 21).* These words prove that you can just continue moving forward and God will show you in which direction you need to go. Take, for instance, the setback with my inflamed hand. Of course I was doubting at that moment whether I was on the right path, but at the same time I really wanted to finish the course. Slowly I was learning that not everything is to be explained as a sign from God.

That would mean that every setback or small success would determine the direction to follow. It could be likened to a cyclist doing the Tour de France turning back each time he was about to climb a mountain because the steep slope would make his calf muscles ache. I was gradually discovering that doing the will of God has everything to do with perseverance and joy. It doesn't only involve going through hard times, it is also about joy. I thought it was wonderful to be learning Spanish and going to Bolivia.

That was the plan and I knew that God was behind it. Sometimes I experienced unpleasant things, and I had to learn how to deal with these. I might then say, 'That's God's will for today.'

Most of the things that God wants for us are written in the Bible. You don't need a revelation or a special calling. If you come across clear guidelines in the Bible, you need to apply them in a practical way. I think that's often where the challenge arises. I have noticed it's hard to discover God's will if you don't get moving. Obedience is the key to faith. You often hear people say they believe in God. James says: "*You believe that there is one God. Good! Even the demons believe that – and shudder." (James 2: 19)* He who believes in God and obeys Him, doesn't have to shudder. Nothing is more exciting than a life lived in obedience to God.

I completed my Spanish course with reasonable marks and was back in The Netherlands in early January 1989. I went from one guest bed to the next, for I no longer had a home of my own.

It had turned out not to be so difficult after all to cancel the tenancy and sell or dispose of all my things. I didn't even miss my little car. However, saying goodbye to Dropje, my little black cat, was terribly difficult. I had become very attached to him, especially during the two years when I was off sick and sitting at home. He was such an affectionate animal and a great support. I found comfort in the thought that to Dropje it did not matter who his master was, as long as his food bowl was filled up at regular intervals.

Now I was back in The Netherlands, I wanted to leave for Bolivia as soon as possible, but I was waiting for financial provision. I had been pretty hard-up in Spain, but after my studies and travels I had no reserves left. In The Netherlands a small support group was prepared to manage the Dutch contacts on my behalf. I had known them for years and like me, they had no experience in this area. There was no close contact with the organisation representing Piet and Marijke. They thought it was fine that I was going to Bolivia, but probably regarded me more like a temporary missionary help to the Punt family.

I was convinced however, that I was not going to Bolivia because I happened to have friends over there, but because I had left a bit of my heart behind. Although I couldn't be certain, I had the feeling that I wouldn't be back any time soon. In fact, my birthday on 25th December that year was probably the last one I celebrated in my native land.

Exactly a year after that special Easter conference in England, on the 10th April 1989, I departed for Bolivia. The money needed to pay for the journey and the first few months of living costs had been provided. This was the decisive moment. At that time, it never crossed my mind that things would develop so fast and that I would be able to make myself understood in Spanish.

On my last night, the farewell meeting was held in a church in Rotterdam, not in Klaaswaal, for my friends and family would have had to travel too far on public transport.

About eighty people came. I was so thankful to share this important moment with them. For my parents, too, it was a special occasion. For the first time they saw how many friends God had given me. Knowing that made it a little easier for them to let me go.

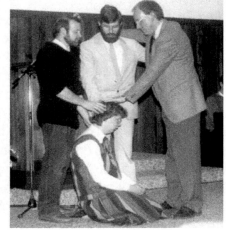

The theme for the talk was taken from Acts chapters 9 and 14. The first passage was about Peter who was used by God to raise Dorcas back to life and the second was about Paul healing a paralysed man. A beautiful message, but I felt like a weak little bird compared to these heroes of faith.

I thought of the various prophecies that had been given to me. I had written them down, but they weren't my motivation. All I knew was that I was available, if God wanted to use me.

Then I remembered that Gert Jan, the pastor of my church, in a vision, had seen me happily sliding down the banister of a large staircase descending from heaven. In the vision I was so happy and wanted to tell everybody how well I was. Then the Lord said He wanted me to change track so that, from then on, I would not live by feelings but by the Holy Spirit. The last words in particular spoke to me, 'On that new track you will not go down, but you will go up the stairs, step by step.' That was what I experienced. In a literal sense, going to Bolivia's high altitude, but also spiritually moving step by step, higher and higher.

Chapter 8

Instant citizenship course

I remember the first time that I ate roast guinea pig. To the Aymara this was a delicacy, whereas to me it was a true ordeal. While I was consuming the small animal, various living specimens were walking round the room, happily whistling and making pleasant sounds. Strange to think that, earlier that morning, my dinner was still walking about. But I mustn't dwell too much on this sort of thing. Anyway, when I went out visiting I no longer asked questions about the things on my plate. Half a cow's head could be staring at you from your bowl of soup while the host gnaws on a jawbone, quite a common sight.

Fortunately, La Paz is a city and you can also get more normal food. There is an abundance of fresh fruit, so don't be concerned that I lacked anything, or that I was constantly disgusted. The visits I made were linked to my work in Peniel, a rehabilitation centre for male addicts. My integration course went much quicker than I could have dreamed. Within a few weeks of arriving in Bolivia, I became involved with this work, which was just right for me. I will tell you how that came about.

I had only just come to La Paz when Juan Clementi held an evangelisation crusade in a cinema in the city centre. Piet and Marijke Punt, with whom I was staying during my first weeks, and I were involved with following up enquirers. One evening, just before we were going to the meeting, Annemiek, Piet and Marijke's daughter, jokingly said, 'Say hello to Juan Clementi for me.' 'Yes, I will,' I blurted out.

Sitting in the bus, I was suddenly reminded of my words to Annemiek and my 'promise'. At first I tried to ignore it, but the thought kept coming back, 'you said you will say hello from Annemiek to the speaker, so you need to keep your word.'

I was dreading it! 'Is that you Lord?' I quietly prayed. Then I thought, 'Oh well, if I must, I will do it,' if only so as not to feel guilty afterwards. So, on entering the cinema, I walked straight to the first row where Juan Clementi was already seated. 'Hello, I am Fineke. You do not know me, but I bring you greetings from Annemiek Punt,' I said in my best Spanish.

Of course, the poor man did not know who I was talking about, but he kindly thanked me. I just stood there, laughing sheepishly and disappeared to the back as soon as I could. The man sitting next to Clementi had also greeted me kindly. When the programme started he turned out to be the star of the night, a singer with an amazing story. At one time he had been an addict, but thanks to the grace of God he had become a new man. He told us that he had come to faith through the work of Peniel. I had not heard of this organisation, except that I had learned at Sunday school that Pniel, as it is called in the Dutch Bible, was the place where Jacob wrestled with the angel. The organisation Peniel turned out to be well known in South America and had been set up in the seventies by a Brazilian pastor in the city of Belo Horizonte. Since then Peniel has grown extensively and now has branches in many countries, even in China.

The singer announced that a Peniel rehabilitation centre had just been opened in La Paz. I was all ears. The new centre was specifically for men wanting to kick their addiction. I thought, 'This is exactly what I have been trained to do.' I had worked with the homeless in London, and during my training my work placement had been in the Hoogeland Stichting in Beekbergen.

Through keeping my promise to greet Juan Clementi before the meeting I had already met the singer. That made it less difficult to walk out to the front afterwards and contact the leadership of

Peniel. When I introduced myself, I was warmly invited to come along.

The leader said, 'You can tell our residents how you came to know Jesus.' I thought, 'That's a strange way of being introduced, but I don't mind, I will just go along.' Straight after the crusade, I went to Peniel and there I found God had opened the way before me. Samuel, the leader whom I had met before, seemed preoccupied.

'We have a problem', he said, sounding confused. 'Another leader and I will be fasting and praying today as we don't know how to take the work forward. It would be good if you share your story with the guys, but we won't be there.' It sounded rather dramatic, so I didn't ask any questions. I was being thrown in at the deep end. Walking to the lounge, I met a number of men and they

reminded me of the Simon Community. Most of them were between twenty and thirty years of age. I told them what I had come for and, to my surprise, they were open to hearing the story of my conversion. From other rooms in the house, more men were invited to come and once they were all there, I started. Of course, I spoke at length about my experiences in London, but also about my  conversion at Rora House. Compared to these men I had been a "good girl", but they were touched by the idea that good girls are also in need of God. I noticed a sense of trust developing. They also understood that I was not looking down on them. I told them how, as a teen, I had discovered that decent people can get into trouble in no time at all. Several men nodded and recognised their own situation. To me this first meeting in Peniel was like a kind of homecoming.

Because the leaders were busy praying, somebody else had

offered to take all the residents on an outing to Lake Titicaca. I was asked to come along as well. I will always remember that day. The weather was brilliant and the lake breathtakingly beautiful with its crystal-clear water and the rugged landscape of the bare hills. Hardly a word was spoken during the first hour. Everyone was enjoying the stillness and the panoramic views.

The lake was dotted with the occasional strangely rigged white sail of a small fishing boat close to the azure blue water.

This change from the drab city benefitted us all. Sitting on the lakeside, I got talking with Juan, a young guy addicted to cocaine. In the past I had only had contact with alcoholics. The fact that, back home and in England, I had found it difficult to have a meaningful conversation with drug addicts was probably because I had not had real contact with them. Juan changed my perceptions.

I realised that his addiction was the consequence of lots of distress, rejection and disappointment with life, and especially the lack of loving care and clear boundaries in his childhood. By the end of that day I was convinced that God had arranged this contact with Peniel. I was asked to give a weekly Bible study and to help with rehabilitation when possible. That was the very thing I wanted to do. You must understand that my involvement with Peniel was not limited to a few hours of Bible study.

When there is a bond with people, time does not matter. The leaders were still dealing with organisational problems. The principle at Peniel is that the leaders are ex-addicts. Of course it isn't easy to lead addicts when you have been an addict yourself. And that profile didn't fit me.

But I think the situation in La Paz is different from Brazil. On the high plain, Bolivians don't find it easy to be under Brazilian leadership, but the Bolivians in the Peniel team lacked the experience to be adequate leaders. I was glad that I was not the only one from a professional background. A young female psychologist called Teresa worked there voluntarily, and we got on well together.

According to another Peniel principle, not only the addicts receive help, but their relatives as well. I thought that was wonderful, even if it did mean eating guinea pig regularly!

Every Peniel work begins as a church, set up especially for ex-addicts and their family members, but welcoming others as well. By coming together in church, turning around and starting a new life, the entire family changes. At least that was the ideal situation. In practice it was not so simple. Most men who were there had hardly any contact with their relatives. Sometimes they had been living rough for years and they could be so committed to that lifestyle that, after weeks in Peniel, they still chose to go back to the street, with the bottle as their only comfort.

Time and again I racked my brains, 'Why do people choose such misery? What is the attraction of that lifestyle? They all know that people are dying daily out on the street, they freeze, fall under a car, catch serious diseases or are gunned down mercilessly.'

I could not understand because I myself was experiencing on a daily basis how God looked after me. At times it even made me feel embarrassed.

I had only been in Bolivia for six weeks when a beautiful little house came up for rent, nicely protected by high walls and situated in the landlady's garden. I say nicely protected, but in this country safety is relative.

You may have high walls to keep burglars out, but here in La Paz there is a very different kind of intruder.

Believe me or not, but I have been visited by 'cacodemons', shapes creeping across my windows like big shadows. I was sure I had closed the gate firmly and that no one was in the court yard, not even the landlady.

You may think I was hallucinating, but when I asked some Christians about this, they were not surprised at all. I had a lot to learn about spiritual things. As I had understood during my first trip, we found ourselves in the very centre of the Indian culture. La Paz and El Alto are riddled with witchcraft, and missionaries in particular are the devil's target. I was cautious and at the same time I knew I was safe in my Heavenly Father's arms.

Apart from the work at Peniel, I had plenty of other demands on my time. I went to the subtropics with Piet and Marijke, where we were invited to speak at a regional church conference of around five hundred people. It took us only eight hours in the car, whereas some participants travelled for over twenty hours. Bolivians are willing to sacrifice a lot to be together as Christians! I was privileged to lead some Bible studies for women.

Another journey took us to the Peruvian border, where we helped at a children's camp for a day. I told a story and I was pleased to notice that my Spanish was all right. The children were all ears.

I still took Spanish lessons, for I wanted to have a better grasp of the grammar. That was especially important because I was hoping to study Aymara at La Paz university. Recently I had also started teaching English at the Bible School of Asambleas de Dios, the church that had invited me to come to Bolivia. According to the students I was doing well, but I think I learned more Spanish from them than they learned English from me.

I began to visit Peniel more frequently. At times I also visited the homes of the families of our residents. I have already told you about my first guinea pig meal, but when you went into their homes you really started to understand the meaning of poverty. This was not only caused by the father's drinking problems. Often it was the vicious cycle of poverty in a society with no opportunity for betterment. Everyone was crowded together in one small room, without running water and without sewerage. Small children went barefoot although most nights, the temperature was below zero. I was really shocked by many people's living conditions. I understood that the majority of Bolivians lived below the poverty line, yet when you strolled around the city centre as a tourist, it was not evident. However, when you moved to the outskirts that were built up against the slopes, poverty was very apparent.

My involvement at Peniel occupied me more than anything else. I think this is how the will of God works. It does not happen consciously, but something grows inside you that makes you go in a certain direction.

A few residents, with whom I had had intensive talks, had left, like twenty-five-year-old Gustavo. I didn't know what had come over him when he unexpectedly went AWOL. Why did he not leave a message? Probably because he knew that we would do everything we could to change his mind. We searched all the places where we thought he might be.

You could find groups of desperate people everywhere, in parks, out on the street, in bushes or begging at the entrance of a church. They were often by themselves during the day but, as evening fell, they usually gathered in groups in search of a place to shelter for the night. Their most valued possession was a plastic fizzy drink bottle containing a mixture of pure alcohol with a bit of lemonade to make it taste better, or a small of bottle of paint thinner or glue.

We could not find Gustavo anywhere. With aching hearts we had to stop our search. A few days later, we received the news that he had been found dead. At such a moment everybody in the centre turned quiet and sombre, each with their own thoughts. I didn't know what the men were thinking. My thoughts went back to those few talks with Gustavo, from which I found that he had been living in an absolute mess for twenty-five years: sexually abused, thrown out of the house, familiar with the most terrible prisons in Bolivia. Who knows how he had met his end?

Carlos Esteban, another resident at Peniel, also left, but with a totally different destination. He went to Cochabamba Bible School in the subtropics. I had spent many hours talking with Carlos. He came to regard me as his mother, and I felt the same bond with him. His own mother had died and because of alcohol he had lost contact with the other members of his family. Carlos had made a new start and the Lord Jesus now ruled his life. His departure for Bible School was a good reason for throwing a party. I hoped to visit him as soon as possible.

Chapter 9

Behind bars

In the middle of town, adjoining a beautiful small park where lovers go walking on warm days and small children are out playing, the big prison of La Paz is situated. Less than fifty yards from this idyllic place fighting, blackmailing, dealing and raping takes place. This is the underworld training centre. When you end up here after a small offence, you can be pretty sure that crime will not let go of you after your release.

Behind the bolt barred gate at the entrance prisoners are waiting for a sign from outside, visiting relatives or a deal to smuggle inside.

Being ushered in through a small gate in the fence, one looks straight into the entrance of a Catholic church. Symbol of the Spanish oppression. I wonder how many Indians have been baptised under duress or were baptised to avoid punishment? The wall surrounding the prison complex must be at least ten metres high, with a gallery on which guards are walking up and down. Except for the wall and the church not much is left now of the original building which was erected by the Spaniards. These days it is a jumble of alley ways, wooden stairs, balustrades and small home-made dwellings. Somewhere in this maze is the small Protestant church of Jonas. Adalit, the pastor, is a prisoner himself who has come to faith by the evangelization activities of others. Together with Carlos Esteban, who has now finished Bible school, I regularly visit this church to give Bible studies and to talk with prisoners.

According to insiders, getting in to the prison outside of visiting hours should be quite a job, but we have not been aware of that.

Maybe because we spoke to the right man at the right time when we made the appointment. Because it is outside of visiting hours,

I am the only woman in a prison complex which holds fifteen hundred criminals, where weapons, drugs and alcohol are traded freely. Yet, on my way to the improvised church I feel fairly safe with Carlos behind me and Adalit in front. While walking up and over the narrow stairs and through dark alley ways, Adalit urges me to walk faster. He keeps looking behind him and keeps the distance between us as small as possible to prevent us from being robbed.

We arrive safely in the 'church hall', put together with sheets of chipboard. When I see the prisoners entering in I don't recognise any of the horrid stories that are going round. I can only see beaten up and defeated people whose eyes are longing for a different life. These people may be criminals but I see they are yearning for recognition and love, and have come specially to listen to the Word of God.

We have come in particular for Juan Carlos, a boy with a terrible background. After an earlier prison sentence, he was taken into Peniel for a short time. Maybe he was too young amongst all those adult guys; he did not stay for long. Now Juan Carlos is in prison again for some offence or other. Today is his fifteenth birthday. We have brought him a present.

He is touched somehow when we meet him and he appreciates our prayers for him. When we tell him emphatically, he can always come back to us, he smiles wryly. We will never judge him for the mistakes he has made. These people have an inbuilt sense of self-condemnation. They feel condemned because they are never welcome, because of ever-absent parents, because the government is only there to put you behind bars and does not help you to a better future. Right now, this lad cannot believe, his view on life is very blurred. However, I hope with all my heart that at some point in time he will be able to receive the love of Jesus into his life.

It will be difficult for him to keep to the prison regime. There are so many unwritten laws, determined by the law of the jungle. The leader is he who exercises greatest authority, fears nobody and has gathered most 'slaves' around him. The influence of this kind of leader is huge: some prisoners would rather remain in prison than be freed. They would hardly cope outside this tough hierarchy inside prison. Some would also prefer to stay inside because in prison the price of drugs is many times lower than outside. Behind these thick walls, in the middle of La Paz, this is a peculiar subculture. I even know some converted prisoners who are dreading their release. They do well with one another in their small prison church, they receive good education, learn to be a witness for Christ. How will that be once they are back on the streets? Which church will give room to the ex-prisoner to be active and grow spiritually?

Carlos Esteban initiated the prison visits. He started when he was at Bible school in Cochabamba. During that period I started to join him. Carlos still sees me as his mother and I think of him as my son. It may sound strange: he is a guy in his twenties, but to him it is very important to talk to me as if I were his mum.

The age gap between us is almost fifteen years, but that does not really matter. He missed so much during his teenage years. I feel responsible for him and I am as proud as a real mother that Carlos started this important work of his own accord.

He is now a member of staff at Peniel. Fancy that. It was only a year ago that he was in deep trouble. Fortunately one does not easily get put on a pedestal, like some former addicts in the Netherlands and the US.

By the way, something beautiful is growing between Carlos and Teresa, the psychologist. I was the first one to know. They are madly in love and I am so happy for these two people. At this moment I am living with Teresa in the rehabilitation centre because director Samuel and his wife are on leave in Brazil.

To be honest, I doubt whether they will return at all. The tension in the team that was there when I first came to Peniel has never really gone. I have been appointed director for now. It is quite a responsibility but fortunately we have a good team that gives themselves one hundred percent to the work.

At Peniel we are short of space. A number of guests have to sleep on the floor. But for them that is no reason to leave. Most men are used to sleeping in a porch or on a hard bench. Reasons for leaving often have to do with addiction or resistance to the gospel. Peniel is an open centre, so we do not hold on to anybody. Of course, we have long talks with those who want to leave, but we cannot hold them. It is a pity that many who leave without having followed the whole programme will not get another chance. That is why we will look everywhere for the one who does a moonlight flit. Such a search may take days on end. It is the only way we can show that we care and that we do not judge.

After many talks Hernan, an eighteen-year-old lad, decided to leave in the end. We searched no end for him, but could not find him anywhere. When we heard that he had been arrested we went to the police cell. He shared a four-by-four metre cell with twenty-five other men, without food and totally disillusioned.

This started off a new branch in the work. We now have permission to take food into all police cells on a weekly basis and we are also allowed to go in and provide people with pastoral care. Often it starts with taking messages from prisoners. 'Will you call my mum and tell her I am here?" or 'I regularly need medicines; please can you buy such and such pills at the chemist's?' The police are not involved with informing relatives and this is how it is: no family - no food.

Unwritten laws are respected by all in police cells. Even the police use social relations that come about amongst detainees.

The leader usually is the one who has been there longest. Newcomers pay him a sum of money in exchange for protection and other privileges. The person who is there for small trespasses pays more than a toughie.

In some cells the inmates think up occult games to generate sufficient income, which means: an adequate number of new detainees. For instance, they will draw a skull on the wall and pierce a hole in the wall for a mouth. As the ritual starts, they will put a burning cigarette in the mouth of the skull. Banging their fists against the wall, they will ask the devil to bring misery to as many people as possible so that the cells will be filled with new folk.

You would think little contact could be made with these hardened guys, yet there is plenty of openness to the gospel in the police cells. Especially amongst the newcomers are rather upset and fear long penalties. The judicial system in Bolivia is unpredictable: a small offence may lead to months behind bars. For many detainees this is the right moment to reflect on their life.

When I was first admitted into a police cell, I sang a rhymed version of Psalm 3 to the twenty-five men, one of which was Hernan. I was surprised to see so many men trying to join in: '*I call out to the LORD, and he answers me from his holy mountain. Arise, LORD! Deliver me, my God!*'

Shortly afterwards I was back in that cell and one of the prisoners enthusiastically started to tell: 'Hermana Fineke, I have seen the Lord Jesus. Over there, in the corner, He was playing the guitar.' At my last visit he had been so drunk that, when he heard that Psalm, he thought the Lord had appeared to him. Besides, a crucifix was hanging behind my head. That was it for him.

Visiting all police cells in La Paz is impossible; there are too many. Therefore, we limit ourselves to the police stations where people are asking for us. During our first visit to one cell twenty prisoners came to know Jesus. We prayed with them and go there every week to give a Bible study.

Of course we don't know how things will go once they are released. Will they keep going to church? Will they keep reading their Bible, even when things are going easy?
We have made an arrangement with Adalit, pastor in the central prison: after people have been transferred from the police cell to prison, he will help them grow in faith.

I do not see myself as an evangelist, but I am convinced that you should not keep people with problems in suspense with nice stories. Some people think that I must allow prisoners more time and space to reflect. But how much space and freedom does someone actually need who has been in prison for weeks or months? Maybe he or she has no time or space left to convert. Of course handing out love is the starting point. A bowl of soup and a bread roll work wonders. It means a lot to a prisoner if I send a message to relatives. But if these people do not know what drives me to do this work, they will not spontaneously think of God. They need to know that only Jesus will enable them to really solve their problems. When we enter the prison or police cell, He comes in with us. I have no ready-made answer to all vital questions, but I am a child of God and love those people. When you meet someone in need, you cannot be silent about God's salvation. It would be similar to a captain refusing to hand out life-jackets on a sinking ship.
With many people hovering between life and death I have shared the gospel in my own inadequate way. Only God knows what happened spiritually in those last minutes before their death.

Even when someone is dead drunk, you can talk about God's love and the good news of Jesus' resurrection. You never know what your words bring about in the other person. Maybe he does not remember any of it, but unconsciously he may have picked up something of the Word. Just like the man in the police cell that mistook me for Jesus.

◆ ◆ ◆

Recently a group of six men came to Peniel. One of them was a young thirteen-year-old boy. I think they used him for burglaries: making him creep through toilet windows and stuff like that.
Who knows what else they did to him. The boy kept missing his mum. We sat in the lounge talking when the boy suddenly came and sat very close to me. Minutes later he put his head on my lap and fell asleep. I could hardly hold back my tears. How this boy missed a loving mother. And I was powerless in this desperate situation.

The little lad was in the clutches of the street gang and even though he trusted me, I was not able to take him away and maybe find another solution for him.

The group was only with us for a couple of days. I think they understood that our programme would upset their group culture and their personal lives considerably. The young boy timidly went with them.

My heart was broken. This was the second teen coming to our centre. I knew that out there hundreds more were walking the streets, acting the tough guy in a group or all alone, but almost always addicted to glue and alcohol.

In all of Bolivia I had not come across a good Christian organisation yet, that would take care of these youngsters.

This was not just an emotion coming over me. Young people had always had a special place in my heart. Of course, in Amersfoort and Middelharnis I had worked with this age group, but on that particular night this boy awoke something that had been slumbering in me for a long time. The idea was being born to open a home for teens. I get excited thinking of what this could mean for the future.

Chapter 10

A shelter in the making

Misión Adulam was started on 6th June 1993. After many months the official papers had finally been signed. The plan was that a boys' home would be set up first, because that was the most urgent need. However, there were no adequate shelters for girls either, so that would probably be the next step.

The name "Adulam" (refuge) is in the Bible. It was name of the cave where David and his men hid from King Saul. The band of men in Adulam was not just made up of people like David, a poet, musician and shepherd. Many of them had some sort of criminal record. But when David became king, these former underdogs were given positions of responsibility in the kingdom of Judah and Israel. I was convinced that the young people who found shelter at Misión Adulam would turn out to be a blessing to Bolivian society. Boys and girls, who were once written off but now were being given a second chance by God's grace, would be an example for the whole country. Hence the name Adulam.

It's odd, but perhaps also characteristic of the Indian culture, that I could not find a good Aymara word for refuge. When Aymara talk about refuge, they mean dodging the law. That was not what I wanted for a Christian organisation.

Because my work at Peniel took a lot of my time, the official start of Misión Adulam was a long while in coming. However, I knew that God had all things in His hand. Meanwhile I had been accepted as an independent missionary with the same Dutch faith mission as Piet and Marijke: Mission and Church.

The name also expresses the vision: to always practise mission from the church. I completely agree with that. Here in Bolivia I can tell when my home church is praying for me or when there is distraction that hinders the focus on missions. In the meantime, Kees and Fieke Goedhart, leaders of Mission and Church, came to visit me.

Unfortunately, Peniel was going through upheavals that I was powerless to prevent. Some Bolivian workers had staged a coup. It was the same old story of national pride and not being able to get over the fact that Peniel was governed from Brazil.
Peniel's Brazilian leaders adhered to the Biblical principle of not suing fellow Christians. I think that was tremendous because the Bolivians had taken over all the assets without paying a penny for them.
Luis, who had been my co-director for some time, started all over again, still under the flag of Peniel-International. Latin-American style scandals also happen among Christians.
I think it was the response of the evil one to the growing prayer movement in Bolivia. A division was emerging between people who really wanted to obey God and those who were after personal gain. It was unclear how this would affect the care provided for addicts. However, the evil one will always reap profit from division among Christians.

These kinds of struggles can ensnare people who have not really broken with their past. For instance, one of the ex-addicts who had rehabilitated in Peniel had started to collect money for another foundation called Adulam, set up by himself. The enemy has a great imagination. Many believed this man was working for me, but nothing was further from the truth. He was putting the money in his own pocket.

He was especially active in Cochabamba, some four hundred kilometres away. I travelled there and confronted him with his problem. My bluntness scared him but he did not want to admit that he was doing anything wrong. I went to his wife and asked her if she wanted to be married to a thief. She was unaware of any of this and was so shocked that she was able to convince her husband to stop.

In my presence he signed a document in which he agreed to forgo further activities under the name of Adulam.

As a single woman in this country, I sometimes need to take a stand. Some assume that I am scared of men. Well, I was not brought up like that. Thankfully, 'my son' Carlos and his wife Teresa were not involved in this hassle. They had been married for a year and had a sweet

Teresa, Carlos Esteban and Stephanie

little girl, Stefanie. So, I had a granddaughter even though I was only thirty-six summers young, far too young to be a grandmother! Less pleasant was the fact that Carlos had started drinking again. Because of self-reproach and shame he did not dare face the truth and that only made matters worse. For anyone who has been addicted at some point in his life continued abstinence is extremely difficult. I did encourage him, but only by phone since they had moved to Santa Cruz, over eight hundred kilometres away. Fortunately Carlos' wife Teresa was a sensible woman, but of course this was not an easy time for her.

To top it all, I went to The Netherlands for three months for a major operation. It was very hard, not only physically, but also emotionally. From now on, I would never be able to have children of my own.

How comforting are God's words in times like these! He knows exactly what we are going through and says: '*I will betroth you to me for ever; I will betroth you in righteousness and justice, in love and compassion. I will betroth you in faithfulness, and you will acknowledge the Lord*' (*Hosea 2:19, 20*).

My work at Peniel was finished and I was free to devote my time to Misión Adulam. I was able to go out on the streets more often, to care for the homeless and build friendships with the teens that we met. During the evening and night shifts, men accompanied me. In the daytime, I usually went with Teresa Perez, who had joined the work at Misión Adulam.

Teresa herself had been through a terribly difficult time and had a compassionate heart for the homeless. Actually, I had known her since I first came to live in Bolivia. Because of his alcohol addiction, her husband was a resident at Peniel for a while. But he was unable to overcome the alcohol addiction and he finally left his wife and two little children, without any income whatsoever. During that same period, after the birth of her second child, Teresa got an aggressive type of rheumatism and was too weak even to feed little Anita. All alone, she was having to watch her children grow thinner by the day. It was at that point that I went to see her. I was shocked and bought her some food that very same day.

This happened a few years ago, but thinking of it still gives me goose bumps. The Sunday after I had taken her the food, Teresa

Teresa

and her little ones came to the meeting at Peniel. She was in tears when she gave her life to Jesus. The changes that followed would forever take away any doubt in Teresa and myself about the question of whether God is able to look after His children.

The first miracle was that little Anita started breastfeeding again and the very thin Diego started growing and thriving.

Another miracle was that the rheumatism became less aggressive. Teresa could manage her own household once more. The thing that may have impressed me most was that the rice and sugar that I had brought never ran out. Despite the fact she used them regularly, the quantity did not lessen. After six months the family still had enough rice and sugar. To me it was evident that God takes care of those who call out to Him in need.

As soon as Teresa was reasonably well again, she started working in the Catholic alms-house Santa Maria, a branch of the world-wide work of beatified Mother Teresa. Teresa was mainly involved in elderly care. She had to work really hard, washing and caring for the infirm old people. She herself says that while she was working so hard, she forgot about her rheumatism. If work permitted, she told her patients about Jesus. As a result, some old people accepted Jesus in their hearts shortly before dying.

The sisters of Santa Maria were not very happy when Teresa left to come and work for Misión Adulam, but the relationship between Adulam and Santa Maria was still good. We were even able to arrange for the sisters to receive a homeless person with severe learning difficulties. Because Teresa had a lot of medical experience, we became more actively interested in the physical condition of the people out on the street. Alcohol, poor and inadequate nourishment, neglect and promiscuous sex caused many homeless people to fall ill. If necessary, and if the patient agreed, we tried to arrange a bed in a hospital. That was easier said than done, though. Taking someone to hospital required a lot of personal involvement.

We soon noticed that having a number of homeless people hospitalised meant we had our work cut out. The nursing staff only did the really necessary jobs, and sometimes not even those. Without family or friends, patients were not guaranteed meals or even medicine. Here are a few real-life stories to help you understand the ins and outs of the healthcare provision in Bolivia.

Felix
Felix smelt like a cesspit. I am used to quite a lot, but talking to Felix nearly made me want to walk away. After having gained a

little bit of his trust, I carefully dared ask him where this awful smell was coming from. He lifted his T-shirt a little and showed me his completely soiled stoma[1]. We asked him when he had last had it cleaned.

With a grin Felix said, 'I think about a year or so ago.' He was clearly not aware of the risks of infection. Straight away we put him in a taxi and went with him to the hospital.
One of the nurses started to laugh loudly at seeing the stoma. She said, 'We have never come across anything like this.' It was clear enough that this situation could not have continued for much longer. There was grit, bits of straw and lots of dirt in it. Fortunately, we had found him in the nick of time.

Felix stayed in the hospital while we were dispatched to buy a colostomy bag and other things needed for the operation. After searching for the supplies at four or five different pharmacies, we returned to the hospital to find Felix had a new neighbour. A man had been brought in and was handcuffed to the bed.

This was the first time we discovered that hospitals are ideal places for making contact with people. In hospital there is ample time to reflect on life. The handcuffed man was eager to talk with us and within fifteen minutes we were able to tell him that he could live a different life and that God was waiting for him to decide.

Renan
Renan was about fifty years old and at one time he had followed the rehabilitation programme.
However, he had started drinking again and had ended up on the streets. During one of our food runs, we found him in El Alto, very, very ill and huddled between some cardboard boxes on the street. He couldn't even communicate, so we called for a taxi and took him to the most basic hospital.
Throughout the journey, Renan was shivering in our arms.

1 *Stoma: A surgically constructed opening in the abdominal wall that permits the passage of waste into a bag.*

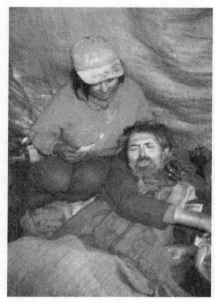
Renan

On arrival in the hospital it turned out there was no bed available, so we left him in the waiting room. After a few hours we returned and found Renan in bed, stark naked, in a ward with three other men. Apparently, he had been infested with lice and the nurses had thrown away his clothes.

We quickly bought some second-hand clothes and dressed the patient, who was shivering violently. Only after Renan had warmed up could we ask him why he was living out on the streets again. 'You spent years rehabilitating in Peniel. How did you get back into the world of alcohol?' 'You are right, I think that was a stupid thing to do,' Renan stammered. He felt deeply ashamed. 'I think you need to tell this to God,' I said rather sternly. 'Have you asked him to forgive you for being disobedient?'

He shook his head and mumbled, 'I want to do that. I want to turn over a new leaf.' 'Shall we pray together,' I asked. He nodded. 'You pray first, for God is your Father and He wants to hear your voice.' He remained silent for a long time, but then he started sobbing, 'God, I am sorry for all the things I have done. Drinking, fighting, stealing, deceiving. Will You forgive me? Amen.'

When all was quiet again, we prayed that God would heal him and help him to keep to the straight and narrow path. The other patients lay there and listened.

After we had finished praying, we heard someone from the far corner in the ward say in a husky voice, 'Please, will you pray for me as well?' I turned round and saw that the man had tears in his eyes. 'Of course we will pray for you'. We went over to him and shook his hand. His name was José Luis.

'What do you want us to pray for, José Luis? Do you know what praying is? Do you know that the God we pray to has given his Son, who has died for your sins?'

José Luis knew nothing about Jesus. We explained the gospel to him. He was deeply impressed and after we had prayed for him, he confessed his sins and asked Jesus to become Lord of his life.

In the bed next to him, an elderly man with a faint voice said, 'What about my sins?' I turned round and explained the gospel to him as well. He, too, wanted me to pray for him and decided to commit his life to God.

It turned out to be one of the most wonderful evenings of the previous few years. I had started to like this and turned to the fourth man and asked him, in a bit of a cheeky way, 'And how about you, do you know the love of God?' The man shook his head. A little while later we prayed with him, and he too committed his life to God.

When I next visited Renan, I gave the new Christians a New Testament. But Renan was too ill. He had been diagnosed with advanced typhoid. The three men picked up their Bibles and started reading straight away.

A few days later José Luis called me over and said, 'Fineke, I read here that Jesus heals people. Does He still do that?'

'Yes, I believe Jesus still heals people.' I answered in a rather offhand manner for, until then, I had never prayed for anyone to be healed. I asked him what his problem was. 'I cannot pee,' the man answered. I realised I could not brush this off, just because I had never prayed with an ill person. After all, Jesus is the healer, I realised. 'Let's pray about it then,' I said.

On the basis of James chapter 5, I explained that it says in the Bible that the sick must be anointed with oil. I had some oil in my handbag and put a few drops on his forehead.

Very simply I prayed, 'Lord, You know I am not a specialist in this area, but please don't let my unbelief be an obstacle if You want to heal José Luis.' We returned to the hospital a few days later and José Luis called out enthusiastically, 'Hermana Fineke, it is ok now. There is nothing wrong anymore.'

Teresa met him again a few months later and heard he was still doing fine.

Medical help for Renan had come too late. He died in hospital. But I think that was God's grace. Renan simply didn't have the strength to keep off the alcohol.

Chapter 11

A place to get clean

At the busiest market in El Alto, I encountered four lads who were fourteen years old at the most. They asked me for money, supposedly to buy a bread roll, but of course that was not really their intention.

'I won't give you money,' I said, 'but I don't mind buying you something.'

'Ok, we would really like a drink,' the eldest one said. Apparently, he was the leader of the group and was trying out a variation on the bread roll trick. We walked over to a stall with a terrace and I ordered four bottles of lemonade. They muttered discontentedly at first but eventually all of them accepted a bottle from me.

I think they found it interesting talking to a foreigner and I invited them to come and sit down.

'What's your name?' one of them asked. I told them who I was and what I had come to do. They were amazed that someone would come all the way to Bolivia with the aim of helping street kids.

'Are there many of you?' I asked curiously.

They nodded, 'Yes, usually dozens of us are out here in the market. We live out on the streets and at night we hang out behind a building next to the motorway. When will you come again? Then you can meet our friends as well.'

A week later the lads took Teresa and me to the place next to the motorway. There we met a group of about twenty-five young people, a small baby and an old granny.

I had visited many groups on the street, some I knew so well they had become friends. Every now and again there was a teenager amongst them, but never before had I seen so many young people

together in one place.

From that moment on we got to know more and more street kids. We came across terrible situations: teens that had sniffed so much glue that their brains had been damaged by the aggressive solvents. Some had not been sober for many years. To earn a little money, many of these young people did odd jobs like washing cars or polishing shoes. The underworld, too, liked to make use of these street kids to do their dirty work. In the best-case scenario, this would mean helping with a burglary, but sometimes it meant getting rid of a rival.

They were a vulnerable group, usually from broken homes. Sometimes they were completely ignorant of their past, because they were abandoned as babies and had grown up in orphanages.

José (on the right in the photo) was a typical example of a boy who got hopelessly caught up in the criminal world. Along with Luis, who leads Peniel, I visited José's youth gang. José was eighteen years old. He was known as the knife

fighter. He had already wounded quite a few people – or worse. This time José was at the end of his tether. We noticed he wanted to express what was bothering him. Despite being under the influence of alcohol, he was reasonably approachable. In the middle of his story he broke down in tears. We asked if we could pray for him. He nodded. As we put our hands on his shoulders, we heard someone calling for him from a hedge. Luis left me with José and went over to ask what was going on.

A few nicely dressed gentlemen were standing there, waiting to hire José to do a gruesome job for them. Luis managed to convince them to leave José alone or else he would report them to the police. They took to their heels as fast as they could. I didn't know if it was wise to bluff like that. When they suspected betrayal, this kind of criminal wouldn't hesitate to shoot and kill a street kid in cold blood.

How I longed to offer a safe shelter to guys like José. After several attempts, we finally found a house that seemed suitable as a boys' home, although it needed a thorough renovation.

In the end, it had been Teresa who had found the place. In one day, she had viewed no fewer than five buildings and she rather liked the last one. When she came home however, she started to waver and thought she had made the wrong judgment.

After a bad night, she rang me the next morning in tears, and told me about her frustrating day. Straight away I went to see the building and I must say that it was much better than I expected. I felt very good about it. You should have seen Teresa! She was smiling all over because all her uncertainty had vanished.

For years I had been in contact with a church in the El Alto district, not far from the house, and I asked Juan Bohorquez, one of the young pastors of this church, to come and have a look. We made an arrangement for later that week. When I arrived, he was waiting for me at the gate.

The moment Juan walked inside, he suddenly stopped. 'Fineke,' he said, 'you won't believe this. Earlier in the week I saw this very courtyard in a vision.

But there was more. In that vision you were digging a deep hole in the middle of this courtyard. I asked you what you were doing. You answered, 'I am digging a water basin in which all the boys who come to this centre can be washed, so that they will be clean again.' Juan is not a dreamer by any means, so it was very special to hear him speak these words.

House of Adulam

During that season we were living in challenging times, not just because of all the work on the boys' home and all that went with it. The interactions with the teenagers could also be quite intense. I will try and tell you about this, even though you may find it hard to understand.

The things that happened were not just ordinary everyday events. It seemed as if God clearly wanted to define the direction for us to take as we began work with teens on the street for real.

I have mentioned quite frequently that Bolivians are familiar with the spirit world. They see good and evil spirits everywhere. And they go to great lengths to please those spirits. It is easy to dismiss this belief in spirits by using words like 'primitive' or 'superstitious'. That was how the church in Bolivia, as elsewhere, often talked about it. The result was that many Christians in Bolivia did not realise that God's enemy was trying to settle down in our souls' hiding places, just to make sure we would not fully commit to God. Adulam had to be a real hiding place. Therefore, all members of the team who came and worked there must be totally reliable, totally clear. There was a great danger that a Bolivian worker might have been influenced one way or another by the occult. Having been a committed member of a church for many years did not prove that such a person was free from dark influences. The evil one often uses unconfessed sins as a pretext for hiding in the soul of a Christian. Without a doubt, this also applied to me. I had noticed that for a long time there were things I dared not confess. For instance, deep in my heart I was still angry with God for the fact that I was on my own, especially as a relationship had been developing between me and a Bolivian fellow Christian. But he had lost interest when he heard I was not be able to have children. Eventually, I asked one of the leaders in our church to pray for me.

What a relief! It marked the beginning of a totally new perspective on my own life. Maybe you will think this a little strange, but I am now married to God. In a marriage, finance is usually taken care of by the husband, so money matters and all other related things I have put totally into God's hands. And I notice that He looks after me just like the best husband I could ever have wished for. I don't mean this in a disrespectful way but, on the contrary, with deep reverence for Him.

He has also given me promises:
"Sing, barren woman, who has never had a baby. Fill the air with song, you who've never experienced childbirth! You're ending up with far more children than all those childbearing women." God says so! *"Clear lots of ground for your tents! Make your tents large. Spread out! Think big! Use plenty of rope, drive the tent pegs deep. You're going to need lots of elbow room for your growing family.(…) For your Maker is your bridegroom." (Isaiah 54, The Message)*

Juan was another example of someone who was set free. He was the young pastor who shared the vision he had been given of our building. Often, he was so tense and frustrated. I once had the privilege to pray for him and guess what happened? He started to laugh uncontrollably as God showed him His love, and was as happy as a child.

The Holy Spirit moved on him in such a powerful way that, on his way home, this 'proper gentleman' Juan, was swaying down the street like a drunk. The memory of this will stay with him for a long

time to come. Deep inside he now knew that God was his Father forever. He could leave his cares with Him, and He would provide the solutions in His perfect timing. At that time Juan also decided to come and work at Adulam.

All who came and worked at Adulam needed to have been touched by God in a deep way, for they would bear responsibility for people who had big problems. You would really get into trouble if you didn't rely on

Juan

Jesus for your security. As a mission worker it is important to have insight into the spiritual world and to know what it is to speak and act with Jesus' authority. A soft approach is doomed to failure in this work. By the way, true love is tough.

More and more I was coming across Christians who realised they were being held back from obeying God by voices, angry thoughts or paralysing fears. I was developing a better understanding of Jesus' command: *"Heal the sick, raise the dead, cleanse those who have leprosy, drive out demons. Freely you have received; freely give." (Matthew 10:8).*

Every week I was meeting desperate people who longed to be freed from these tormentors. If a person acknowledged that Jesus died for his sins, and confessed his sins to God, then all that was left to do was to send away the demons in the Name of Jesus.

Sometimes they might grumble or attempt various antics to scare you. But still today, all power in heaven and on earth belongs to Jesus.

Maybe you think I have presented this far too simply. The message of Jesus is not complicated. The simplicity of it all is that no one can heal the sick, raise the dead and cast out evil spirits, no one except Jesus. He has shown that He can do this. He gave power to his disciples to do these works in His Name (Matthew 10:1). That makes the command a lot simpler. If, being a disciple of Jesus, you do not act under His authority, you cannot achieve anything. *"Freely you have received, freely give."*

In the previous few months it seemed as if God was preparing us to act increasingly in His authority. Don't forget that the young people we were in contact with were often bewitched, and many of them had been abused or cursed. All of them were addicted to alcohol and drugs, both physically and spiritually. We were no match for these powers unless we received the authority of Jesus. My training as a social worker and my experience in the field of care for addicts and youth was a sound basis for this work, but no more than that. The Holy Spirit would have to do the real work.

How is it that not only unbelievers but also some Christians are enslaved by the evil one? Look at it rationally: no person has a perfect past. There may be sins carried down from our ancestors, there is our own unconfessed sin, traumatic experiences, distress that has not been dealt with or other dark things that may have given entry to the evil one. If that is the case and you want to be delivered, then you first have to confess the sins that stand between God and you, for only then has the evil one no right to remain within you. For he knows that if you confess your sins, you will be washed clean by the blood of the Lord Jesus. In some cases of persistent family sins or deep traumatic wounds, help from the church is often necessary to command the evil one in the Name of Jesus to leave a person. This ministry is called exorcism or pastoral care that sets people free.

When I became a missionary, I knew nothing about these things.

I only found out after contact with my friends in Bolivia and the Netherlands.

In particular, my Aymara friend Beatriz taught me a lot about the spiritual world. She also taught our team on this subject.

Beatriz became my prayer partner. I had known her since the beginning of my days in Bolivia. She is a very modest person, but has a deep insight into the spiritual world, although she will never say that. Since knowing people like Beatriz, my eyes have been opened to the need that arises when evil powers take possession

Beatriz

of people. This is not just experienced by Bolivian people, but by the level-headed Dutch as well. I think people make this issue far too complicated.

Some think spirits are mystical, some say they are a thing of the past, and others go overboard and detect the work of the devil in everything. But, as always, the truth is somewhere in the middle.

Unfortunately, I have had to learn these things the hard way, since I was not at all prepared when I came to Bolivia. Regularly, I stand face-to-face with demon-possessed gang leaders.

They manipulate, laugh and make jokes, but at the same time they are bewitching a whole group of vulnerable, dependant people.

I always remain friendly but on guard as I know a hostile spirit inhabits a person like that. Jesus is the good Shepherd who is in search of those lost sheep.

In the Name of Jesus, we can free the sheep from the claws of spiritual thieves and robbers, not in a heroic manner or with tough language, but simply by staying close to Jesus.

Johnny

Johnny is one of those who was set free. He is one of my spiritual children and now part of the Adulam team.

Johnny's background is similar to that of most boys who come and find shelter in Adulam.

I would like to let him tell his own story:

I come from Santa Cruz and grew up in a family of eight children.

My mother is still alive, but my dad has died. When I was about eleven years old, things at home got completely out of hand. My dad was fired and started drinking. My mum was sick and started drinking with him. By this stage, I had already been through a lot. One little brother had suffocated after my mum had fallen on top of him during an epileptic fit. Once, when I was asked to look after the younger ones because my mum and dad were drunk again, another

little brother died. I always thought that it was my fault. Now I know that isn't true. I didn't want to look after the kids any longer and as a teenager I started to roam the streets. A few lads my age and I started to buy and sell all sorts of things. And with the money we made, we made more money. We never had enough, so we started stealing. Up until I was fifteen it was more like a game, but after that it became serious. I became an experienced thief and more and more I experimented with drugs. First hashish, then the more serious stuff like cocaine. It was going from bad to worse and deep in my heart my anger and hatred grew towards my parents, against everything and everybody.

Deep inside I felt abandoned and cursed. Why was it that my parents were drunkards? Why was it that my little brothers died, one after the other? In the end I was the only one who was left. I cursed my life. I cursed my parents. What had they done to me? Why was I still alive?
I was so good? Was I not a criminal who did everything that God forbade? I was always ready for a fight and wouldn't stop until my victim was beaten to a pulp.

When I was a small eight-year-old boy somebody had told me about Jesus. I had never forgotten that moment, but didn't do anything with it. Twelve years on, shortly before I came to Peniel, some family members took me to a pop concert. I was stoned, so I didn't realise that it was a Christian band playing. I quite liked the music, but hardly listened to the words. Until they sang a song that somehow touched my heart.
At that moment I couldn't stop the tears. I was no longer in control and I saw all the bad things I had done pass in front of my eyes as if in a film: thieving, violence, prison. I felt all the pain, the suffering, the disappointments and I asked God, 'Can you really forgive all that I have done?'
It was as if I clearly heard God's answer, 'Yes, I can.' At that instant I was flooded with love, God's love. It was so overwhelming. I will never forget that moment.

That was not the end of the misery, however. In an increasingly aggressive way, the devil tried to make me believe that there was no forgiveness for me. It became so bad that I tried to take my own life. In the end the devil managed to seduce me into making a pact with him. I promised to be loyal to him and said I would do anything he asked me to if, in return, he would get me out of trouble.

Shortly after, that I came to Peniel in La Paz. I was completely exhausted and had been drinking again. It was Christmas time. Fineke gave me a present and said, 'Go and get some sleep. You can rest now from all your struggles.'

That night the devil returned and said, 'You are mine and that is why I'm going to kill you and swallow you up, so that you will be totally mine. They will never forgive you here for what you have done.' That was the last showdown. For in my bed at Peniel I was given the strength to answer the devil, 'I am not yours, I belong to Jesus, and His blood has cleansed me from all my sin. I now live here in Peniel and I don't care whether I have to start my life all over again, from the bottom upwards.'

I cried out to God and it was as if He spoke to me. I heard the question, 'What did Moses have in his hand when he made a way through the sea so that he could flee the enemy?'
I replied, 'A rod.' 'And you, what have you got?'
I answered, 'The Name of Jesus and the Blood that cleanses every sin'. Then it was as if I heard God say, 'Use it!'
Then I said, 'In the Name of Jesus, I belong to Jesus'.
And to the devil I said, 'You be quiet!'
I was sweating, but became as quiet as a baby in his mother's arms. I got up and walked over to the patio where people were still celebrating Christmas. They were singing about Jesus and I cried out, 'Thank you, Lord God!'

Later, Fineke read me a passage from Scripture that touched me deeply: "*When I shut up the heavens so that there is no rain, or command locusts to devour the land or send a plague among my people, if my people, who are called by my Name, will humble themselves and pray and seek my face and turn from their wicked ways, then I will hear from heaven, and I will forgive their sin and will heal their land.*" (2 Chronicles 7: 13,14)

I had been living in sin and God had shut up the heavens and the locusts had had full sway. But the moment I started searching for

God and confessed my sins, He forgave everything and started to "heal the land".

Johnny's story is a wonderful testimony of God's grace and mercy. The next chapter continues to reveal more of God's purposes as the ministry in Bolivia developed.

Chapter 12

Choosing a future

The story continues and it was now autumn 1997. Friends living in Holland found it inconceivable that, two years after the purchase of the boys' home, the renovation was still not finished. The architect and the builder had really let us down. Fortunately, many kind people were helping us to rectify the things that had not been done properly, and together we finished the building work. Sometimes I felt like a building supervisor. The advantage is that I can now faultlessly read floor plans and I am an expert in how things should *not* be done.

In Adulam there was room for about twenty boys from the street. We decided not to wait until the building was finished. Fourteen-year-old Alvaro was our first resident, then came Luis who was seventeen and Miguel who was sixteen. The latter two didn't really know their ages. They had no parents and no birth certificates. We assumed they were as old as they said they were and we then had to pick a date to celebrate their birthdays.

The boys who came to us were not asked to do building work. This was not only because they had no relevant training, but also to prevent gossip in the neighbourhood that we used them for slave labour purposes. Nevertheless, street kids were considered the lowest of the low. Quite near to us neighbours hung a life-sized rag doll on a high post with a notice saying: 'This is what  happens to any homeless person who is found up to anything over here.' The boys really felt rejected, not only by their families, but also by society. We didn't want to add to that. We were not running a hotel, but there was love and respect for all that were in need of help.

Of course it was frustrating that the building work was taking so long, but on the other hand this long initial period gained us more and more friends among the girls and boys living on the street. We  could not offer them a roof over their heads, but we had come into their lives. We shared out food and clothing and cared for them when they were sick. In this way we really gained their trust.

At last, the boys' home opened and we could offer a place to those who wanted it. Right from the very beginning of this work we knew that not all of them would want to come. Sharing out clothes and food is usually not a problem, but not everyone wants real help with regards to the future. That's why Adulam was not immediately filled to capacity with young people from the street. In coming to us they had to make choices about education, work and the future.

An adult addict would have had difficulty with these decisions, let alone a teenage addict who lived from one trip to the next. Most of them had never learned to think about the future. Of course, the door was wide open for every young man who wanted to come to us, but that did not mean he would be willing to give up his old life. These are some of their stories.

Marco Antonio

Marco Antonio was sixteen and had only just run away from home. His mother was upset when she came and told us that Marco Antonio did not come home anymore and was roaming the streets. Juan and I spent a long time looking for him. In the end we found him with a rather aggressive street gang. He refused to come with us and we noticed that one of the other gang members was exerting spiritual control over him. In the meantime, the hatred he felt towards his mother had deepened to such an extent we could not talk any sense into his head. Saddened, we returned home, knelt down and together asked God to free Marco Antonio from the power of the group and especially from this man who had such a hold over him. We could do no more at that moment. Whenever we met him, we reminded him of our talk and of course we continued to pray for him.

Edwin and Robby

The events of one particular week showed that working with

teenagers was very different from working with adults.

Edwin (15) and Robby (17) jumped out of our first-floor window with a good number of blankets that they then sold in the street for a quarter of the real price. Afterwards Edwin remorsefully returned to us twice. We did not admit him right away, but only after we had had a straight talk with him. Robby (2nd on the right) came back as well, but we didn't know how long for. Not only was he a danger to himself, he was a danger to us as well. He threatened to blow up the house and in view of his past he was well able to carry out his threat.

We held a vigil for five nights. Looking back, that worked out very positively because it gave us time to pray and made us grow together more as a team. Meanwhile, Robby kept quiet.

There was a positive atmosphere in the house and that was reliant mainly on the staff. Tensions among staff had an immediate impact on the boys.

Robby was one of those who was particularly sensitive to the atmosphere. He liked to shock people. Sometimes we didn't know whether his stories were fabrications or whether he was telling the truth. For example, the time when he happened to mention that he had killed two people. He also claimed that he made a pact with the devil during a satanic ritual, where he had to drink the blood of animals. To make it even more mysterious, he told us satanists or witches had implanted a fetish in his leg.

Though we were not quite sure about all of this, there was no doubt that this boy was severely oppressed by the devil. It was sad to let him go without being changed. We arranged for him to join the military, but once he was there, he chased a sergeant with a knife. So that was the end of that.

Joe

Like the first boys who came to live with us, Joe didn't know his date of birth. He said very little about himself. We assumed Joe was about fourteen years old. He was literally found in the gutter, dead drunk, with a note round his neck which said: 'If we see you once more, you're dead.' When Joe regained consciousness in Adulam, he was terribly aggressive. He didn't mind staying, but was as silent as the grave and continued to behave aggressively. Gradually trust began to grow and little by little he  told us about his background. It was clear that Joe came from the area bordering Brazil.

As a five-year-old he apparently witnessed his parents being shot dead. He then went to live at a cousin's with his sister who was forced into prostitution and was abused sexually by this cousin. She died in horrific circumstances. Joe then walked out and arrived in La Paz after extensive wanderings and encounters with all sorts of shady characters.

Ernan

This lad was sixteen and had himself made the decision to come to our centre and ask for help. One would then have expected him to be motivated to change. However, Ernan was not doing well. For many weeks he was severely depressed. Subsequently, he smuggled alcohol into the centre on several occasions. It started when he had to go to the dentist and met someone he knew on the way back to the mission. Without any thought for the lad's feelings, the man spoke to him, saying, 'Hey Ernan, where have you been all this time? Your mother died last month.'

The poor boy came home to us in a bewildered and damaged state. When he first came to us, he had fled his father. He was so terrified of this man that he made us promise solemnly that we would not tell anybody that he was staying with us. His mother was the only person at home who understood him. And now she had died unexpectedly and he had not been able to say goodbye to her. I could understand how difficult it was for this lad to handle the loss of his mother. It strengthened his feeling that the whole world had abandoned him.

With his mentor, Ernan went to the cemetery, but that didn't really help. He found it difficult to pick up the thread of his life again. And he had been doing so well. A few days afterwards I told him, 'Ernan, if you want to honour your mother, you must pick up your school work and work at your future.'

We went through many intense and heart-wrenching experiences. Over a period of six weeks, ten of our friends from the street died, young ones as well as older ones. Nestor was in hospital with severe stab wounds in his abdomen because he wanted to protect a girl as someone was trying to steal her baby. He didn't know that we had just buried his wife. Ricardo had died and so had Pedro. Graciela was beaten within an inch of her life during a theft and later died of her injuries. I could go on and on. They were all people whom God loved so dearly that for them He sent his only Son into the world. Some of them believed before they died, and some rejected Him. That day I cried uncontrollably after so much grief and, from the depths of my heart, I asked God, 'Lord, how much more do I need to bear?'

The answer came and quietness and peace filled my heart, *'The more you are willing to feel the pain in My heart about the injustice and misery of the people, the more I will give you strength to bear it.'*

As you will appreciate, the dead must be buried. So over time we

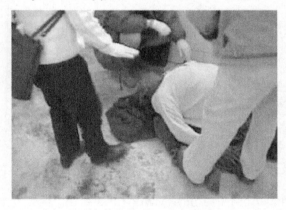

were given another new task. We regularly visited the mortuary to collect and bury a friend from the streets who had died. This didn't happen as discreetly as was the practice in The Netherlands. The dead who had no family or had not been identified were spread out on the floor, sometimes naked and their mutilated bodies lying in a puddle of dried-up blood.

When the police had released the body to us, we would order a coffin and a car from the cheapest undertakers. We would dress our friend in decent clothes and put the body in the coffin. And off we went, straight across town, being held up in traffic jams, via narrow streets and market stalls where vendors were loudly advertising their goods, to the central cemetery. We would quickly buy a bunch of flowers in the market opposite the entrance, find a trolley, (usually done by a few boys to earn a little money) and then locate the right grave number. In the Bible it tells about the man in the land of the Gerasenes who lived in the tombs. That's what it was like for the dead in Bolivia. The coffin was pushed into a square hole.

You can best compare it to the wall of luggage lockers at a large airport, but instead of having a door, the opening is bricked up. Usually the man with the bucket of mortar was waiting for us when we arrived with the

coffin. When he had done his job, we engraved the name of the dead friend in the soft mortar with a piece of wood. 'Our grave' was a poor man's grave, without a glass door, or a marble slab and gilt lettering. Our dead didn't have fresh flowers every week. We put some roses in a jam jar and weighted it with a stone. That was the end of the funeral.

Sometimes a few friends from the street were there as well, in which case I would read a passage from the Bible. Usually there was nobody else, just one or two people from Adulam and the bricklayer.

In Bolivia the difference between a poor man's funeral and a normal funeral is huge. Catholics, in particular, adhere to a clearly-defined death culture: mass after eight days, another mass after a month, another one after three months and again after one year, not to mention making sure there are always fresh flowers on the grave. The balance has shifted completely. Death plays such a central role in the lives of Bolivians that it is no longer considered to be an enemy.

The psychological effect is that people become passive and apathetic and will hardly fight for life. Death, after all, is one's destination, so better keep on the right side of it. Old pagan rituals play an important role, of course. I guess this extreme emphasis on the culture around death makes people feel less responsible for their own life and the lives of their fellow men. I see it also in my friends out on the street. They don't shy away from death at all. They grab a bottle and drink so much that they forget they might freeze to death that very night.

Vincente, an old friend from the streets, had given his life to God, but wouldn't even contemplate giving up drinking or living out on the street. He was in his fifties and had resigned himself to the fact that he would die on the street. He was certain about two things: he would go to heaven and we would give him a burial. Once I went out to find him to tell him I was going on leave to Holland. As we said goodbye he said, 'Fineke, if I die before you do, I will hang up some plastic sheeting for you, so that in heaven you can come and live with me.' Of course it is gratifying

Vicente

to hear someone say that, but at the same time it is distressing to think that even a Christian can be so resigned and not fight for life. The Bible says that death is our last enemy. Because Jesus has conquered it, we need not be afraid of it any longer, but it does remain our enemy. Having the wrong view of death also encourages people try to contact the dead or, when a loved one dies, they find it hard to carry on living.

Especially among the elderly, I know dozens of homeless people who became dependent on drink after their wife, mother or child died. I once met someone who started to weep uncontrollably when he saw me coming. I walked up to him and put my hand on his shoulder. After he had calmed down a little, I asked him what was wrong. He sobbed, 'My mother has died.' I said, 'How sad! When did she die?'

'Ten years ago.' I couldn't believe my ears and had to suppress my laughter. Carefully I tried to encourage him, but I don't know if I got through to him. Naturally one misses one's mother and she cannot be replaced, but to get in a state like that after ten years! The life goes on and one forms new relationships. Some people let themselves be ruled by the past and by death.

Of course we didn't only deal with urban youth who were articulate and persuasive. Bolivia is an agricultural country, and farmers are the backbone of society. Potatoes originated from this area. Since the growth of drug production based on coca, poor farmers turned to growing more and more coca, an old established crop which, in Bolivia, is mainly used for tea and as a kind of chewing tobacco. Then rich countries put pressure on the Bolivian government to stop growing coca plants. That meant a loss of income for many farmers which resulted in them moving to the city in search of alternative work.

In Adulam we regularly dealt with boys from farming families. At home the family often spoke only Aymara. When those boys went to school in the city and learned Spanish, this caused a huge rift between parents and children.

Lucio

Lucio had recently joined us, a fourteen-year-old lad who had travelled from the country to La Paz all by himself. The police brought him to us, because they had noticed him sitting in a doorway for three days. Each time they spoke to him, he started crying. The boy was very upset and had probably not eaten for a whole week. Lucio didn't speak Spanish at all, but that didn't bother us. In Adulam almost everybody spoke Aymara.

A little later we would piece together Lucio's jumbled story. Sometimes he sang softly in Aymara. The other guys thought he was disturbed but, listening carefully, you could hear he was singing about the world of nature and about his own life.

Lucio was a real country boy. He had never seen a toilet before, or a fork. To start with, he would sit for hours in a fetal position in the yard, scratching the loose soil. Maybe this reminded him of his childhood, life on the farm and the dusty fields in the mountains. We didn't know what to do with him. He was not addicted, but we couldn't just turn him out.

After some time it became clear that Lucio had been sexually abused by a woman and he assumed he was the father of her child. His mother had beaten his little brother to death and two other brothers had been sold. His father may have raped a younger sister.

It was likely that Lucio's parents had been deprived of parental rights for he had been living in a home run by the state before he came to La Paz. There he was severely bullied because he only spoke Aymara. So he fled with another boy. They slept in a dog kennel near the state home for a few nights, until the coast was clear. They then walked the long road over the plateau to La Paz. Though he was not addicted, Lucio needed just as much care as the others.

Going to school was not easy. Lucio was admitted to year one in junior school. He didn't do well – not only because he was now one of the little ones but also because he could be very self-willed and was not used to learning.

At Adulam he was often to be seen pottering about, or making small chipboard model houses. His dream was to have a house to himself, a safe place to be. The saddest thing was this: Lucio had never been drunk, not until he came into contact with a slippery character in our home who talked him into coming along to a street gang. There he got drunk for the first time. That week Lucio did not come back to us.

A new world opened up for him. Roaming the streets of the city of La Paz for days on end. Being free. Window shopping, watching people.

At our facility, there was not much to interest a country boy. Later he tried to come back twice, but it became increasingly difficult to accommodate him in Adulam. He was so contrary, so self-willed. Thankfully he is now in a Catholic home with few rules where the boys can do simple work. In the end it seemed that school and Lucio were not a good match.

Chapter 13

No such thing as tough guys

Adulam has fitness equipment, including weights. Of course, every new resident felt the need to display his muscle strength on this 'test' apparatus. The machos among the boys wanted to command the respect of the weaker boys. There was always a lot of masculine pride evident around the dumb-bells. Out of the corner of my eye I could see how, yet again, Jorge and Marcello were busy assessing their strength. I wasn't obviously paying attention, for that would only make them put themselves out even more. And I would have to join in. Over in the other corner I could see thirteen-year-old Johnny surreptitiously rolling up the sleeve on his left arm.  He looked round to make sure nobody was looking, then, with his right hand, checked out his developing muscles. It was a touching scene. Johnny was a quiet, unassuming lad. And when someone like Jorge saw his chance, he would do everything to bully little Johnny. They all had their own way of seeking attention. We let them know that we loved them all equally. When you gave a boy like Johnny a pat on the back, he would come and sit beside you, just like a little boy. He would really have loved to come and sit on your lap, but because those tough guys were around, he couldn't. In reality, these boys were only tough when others were present. Each of them really had a huge need just to be a child. Childhood had been stolen from most of them at a very early age. It was surprising to see how often the box of Lego was pulled out of the cupboard. We thought it was very important for them to catch up a little on their lost childhood. Football was a great favourite, just as it was in The Netherlands. They played many a game of football in the yard. To try and prevent windows being broken, we also provided a table football game. You could tell the enthusiasm of the players by the worn-out wooden figures.

Joe, who had been so aggressive at the beginning, was doing very well. He learned quickly but, more importantly, he really wanted to know the Lord Jesus. In his own way he had decided he wanted to follow Him and his life showed it. He became less hot-headed and at times he was a real example to the other boys.

Every now and again he brought friends home from school. They were in for a surprise when they saw how those so-called street urchins treated one another at Adulam. Their parents had often told them different stories and warned them about those Adulam boys. A few times, one or other of Joe's school friends came to know the Lord. At one point I overheard him say to a new friend, 'You should have a word with Fineke.' I approached them to ask him why he had said that. 'Fineke,' he said excitedly, 'he has been playing with a Ouija board. Will you tell him why that is dangerous?' 'Do you know what a Ouija board is?' I asked the young boy. 'No, not really, but it is exciting,' he replied.
'Yes, I think a burning house is very exciting to watch as well,' I said. 'Would you like to see that?' He answered, 'No, no!'
'And would you like to see inside a burning house?'
'No, that's even more dangerous.' 'Well, actually a Ouija board is even more dangerous. It's like you crawling into a burning house and then asking the person who started the fire how to get out. The Ouija board brings you into contact with demons. Their advice is dangerous. It seems exciting, but you are risking your life.'

Shocked, the boy looked at me. He understood I was speaking the truth. Together we prayed that the demons would not get a hold on his life and that he would become a child of God.

Joe was prepared to bring boys from school back home to Adulam, because the attitudes that prevailed on the street were not brought inside. Newcomers were not allowed to dominate others. If someone thought he was too tough to join the others playing marbles, he might well be given a stiff talking-to. The same would apply to a boy who jeered at those competing to knot the nicest wristband. We were not softies, but the street culture stopped at our front door.

We tried to provide things that teenagers enjoyed, such as swimming or mountain climbing. When at home, we liked to have

a warm, family atmosphere. Sometimes we fancied cooking: una sonsera was always a surprising dish which meant something silly.

Newcomers would be surprised, on asking 'What are you going to make?' when the boys replied in one voice, una sonsera! Two or three would get up at once to come and help me. Out of curiosity, the newcomers came with us to the kitchen and kept asking about 'una sonsera'.

'If you want to know what 'una sonsera' is, you could help by fetching chocolate sprinkles or paprika or yoghurt. It doesn't really matter what you choose.' 'Don't be so silly,' they would say. 'Exactly, that's what it's called. You just wait till you taste it.'

Then I'd let them gather together all kinds of ingredients and throw them all in one pan. The super-meal, una sonsera, always turned out differently and we had great fun. Staying up all night was something they found really awesome.

At the boys' request, we held an all-night prayer meeting from time to time. The first meeting was after the notorious 9/11 attacks on New York and Washington. I was always amazed by the earnestness and frankness of the boys when it came to prayer. A boy who has been kicked out of the house by his father would ask for prayer for his father. At times I couldn't hold back my tears when the boys were praying. There was no need to explain to these boys that praying was important. They experienced from day to day that prayer gave their lives meaning and purpose. We didn't only pray, we sang a lot and ate a big meal in the middle of the night. And they sang beautifully as well.

Of course, all-night prayer meetings were voluntary. If one of them preferred to stay in his room then that was fine. However, most of them liked joining in. Praying together was the best way to get to know these teenagers. New members of staff found the prayers of our boys a real eye-opener. Bolivians on the high plain don't easily show their feelings, certainly not about faith. But these street kids were not bothered at all.

I hardly dare say it, but the official opening of the boys' home was on the 18th of April 1998, two and a half years after we purchased it. The boys found it a bit of a difficult day, with all those guests. But it was important that the local government, the people of the neighbourhood and the people from the church supporting the work were involved on such a day. I hoped the construction of the girls' home would run more smoothly. Our need for that was great and it would have been disastrous if we had to care for the girls, and in particular young mums with children, right in the middle of renovation and building works.

At this time there were some changes in my personal circumstances. First of all, I moved into a house a little closer to the centre of La Paz.

Secondly, I was able to buy my first car, an old Toyota jeep, with the help of churches from the UK and Ireland. It was not very comfortable, but good enough to drive around on the bumpy roads of La Paz and El Alto. I was fed up making those journeys by public transport, travelling along that long road to the top, as we call the journey from La Paz to El Alto. Quite regularly I was called out in the evening or at night because the boys had been up to something and firm action was needed. Then it was no fun having to take a taxi to the top in the middle of the night. Unfortunately, at that stage my authority was respected above the authority of the Bolivian workers. In time, that would definitely have to change.

I had a difficult emotional experience at this time too. Nelson, the young son of friends in my church, became seriously ill and died. This was the first formal funeral service I had ever taken. While Nelson was in hospital, I got talking to a woman who was waiting for her little one outside the operating theatre. All by herself, she had come from the tropics to La Paz for her child's operation. Normally the kitchen of the hospital would have provided meals for her and her child, but following the operation the child needed to be on a drip for a few days. That meant no meals for the mother either.

Because I was visiting Nelson every day, I offered to bring food and drink for the woman for as long as was needed. She gratefully accepted my offer, so I regularly saw her while she was sitting with her little boy.

In the next cot was a baby, without clothes and with a large bandage round its head. The mattress was soaked through. I asked my new friend if she knew whether the baby had a mother. 'No,' she answered, 'it was found in a dustbin and was taken to a government institution.' Moments later, the nurse came in and I asked why the baby was lying there in that condition.

'Oh, it has no clothes,' she casually replied.

Slightly irritated, I said, 'Then I'll go and fetch some.'

I went home, took the smallest items I could find from a box of spare children's clothes, then returned and dressed the little one. Above the cot was a board with the name Carlos on it. A bit abruptly I said to the nurse, 'Right, Carlos is dressed. Now I'm going to feed him.' The nurse got the message, went out, came back and handed me a bottle of milk. Little Carlos had been operated on for hydrocephalus. His arms were as thin as my little finger.

I promised myself that I would take care of Carlos for as long as he lived. Quietly I dedicated him to the Lord. I kept praying for him, even when I was not in the hospital. But Carlos' condition deteriorated quickly. After a few days he stopped drinking. He was very weak, and I think he was blind as well since he didn't respond at all to my movements. I realised his chances of survival were very slim and knew I had to hand him back to the Lord.

Twelve hours later Carlos died.

I often remember him. How happy he must be now!

Chapter 14

Girls on the streets

As more and more boys came to live in Adulam, at the same time, the work on the streets continued. In addition, we continued to visit our friends in the most basic hospital.

The plan to build a home not only for boys, but also for girls dated back to the time that Misión Adulam was first established. Fewer girls than boys lived on the streets, but the need among women and girls was just as urgent. Almost every street gang had some female members. Their lives were even more controlled by the group than those of the boys. If they were not taken under the protection of a male, they were vulnerable to sexual abuse by all of the group. Jealousy, serious rows and frequent violence erupt as men try to steal women from one another. These teenage girls often had one or more children and had also gone through many miscarriages and abortions.

Estella and Heidi

Recently, we were with a group of homeless people, where Estella was the only woman. Her small baby girl, Heidi, was about a year old. Heidi was screaming with hunger and Estella was nowhere to be seen. We asked the man, who claimed to be the father, where she was. 'I don't know,' he said gruffly, 'we were having an argument this morning and she walked off in a huff.'

We took the little one and gave her small chunks of bread which we had dunked in coffee. That was all we had.

The little girl tried her utmost to writhe herself loose from our arms. She kicked and lashed out wildly, especially when Teresa and I tried to pray for her.

Estella and Heidi

Does it sound like an exaggeration when I say that an infant like that can already be under the influence of the wicked one? I myself don't doubt it, especially since she completely quieted down in my arms after we had rebuked the evil one in the Name of Jesus. How terrible to have to leave such a small child behind. Estella (left on the photo, with Heidi) appeared after a while, but being a teenager she didn't really know how to look after her little girl. When Heidi started crying, Estella held a handkerchief with glue under her little nose to make her quiet again. At the age of eighteen months, Heidi died. Her bronchial tubes were completely burnt. God took her home to be with Him.

Monica

It was becoming increasingly clear that the need for a house for girls was urgent. Monica's story focussed our thinking. She belonged to a very aggressive street gang.

When we found her, she had been beaten up and she was pregnant.

The man she was sleeping with had battered her with stones and done all sorts of horrific things.

It was absolutely devastating. On an improvised stretcher, we took her down narrow alleyways and steep mud paths to the car. We drove her to the hospital where she also was diagnosed with cholera.

Several times in the past, I had talked with Monica about the possibility of leaving the street gang and now she lay there, severely wounded and critically ill. Her large, dark eyes looked at me and seemed to be saying, 'I want to stay with you for ever.' I could have burst into tears, but didn't want to upset her even more. With all of my heart I quietly prayed, 'Please, Lord, give me a place where I can take care of Monica, or take her home to be with you.' Monica died fairly soon after that. She was not even twenty years old. So lonely and desolate, so unwanted. She had never known love.

For a social worker it is a terrible thing to have to admit that for a young woman like Monica there is only one place where she is better off: in Heaven.

On the night she died I was with her until about 10 pm. She died at half past five in the morning. The nurse looking after her was a Christian and, in a vision, she had seen Monica leave her body; dressed in white. Monica went to be with Jesus. I had only known her for two years, but He had known her from her mother's womb. Like Monica, many, many girls asked us, 'When will this house for us be ready?' After Monica died, our team started to pray specifically for this.

Five years after Monica died the Lord answered our prayers in a wonderful way. First the boys' home had to be built. And you know how slowly it all went.

On the 23rd of February 2002 Talita Cumi, the house for girls, was officially opened. It was not a renovation, but a brand-new building, painted pure white. The actual building took a mere three months. (What a contrast to the work on the boys' house.) Six months from the date we signed the purchase deed for the plot of land, we held the official opening with the Mayor of El Alto, the Dutch Ambassador, Kees and Fieke Goedhart our mission leaders from Holland, John and Jan Britton from the UK and a number of other people from the area and the church.

It was a huge celebration in which God was honoured most of all. The financial support given by the Dutch Embassy was particularly significant as it enabled us to pay up front for the construction process.

We named the house after the Aramaic words that Jesus spoke to Jairus' little girl: *"Talita Cumi. Little girl, I tell you, rise up" (Mark 5:41).* One day Monica will rise, as well as Olga and Martha and all other homeless people, young and old, who we carried to the grave.

The name Talita Cumi is especially important for the young women who are spiritually dead because of sin and addiction, who are blinded to God's love due to physical and sexual abuse and rejection.

Right from the start the girls' house was well occupied. Yet there were still many girls on the street who dared not come. It was difficult to free yourself from the grip of the gang. But maybe, in the end, it would become easier, though I sometimes didn't understand what held them back.

Take Maria, for instance. She lived around the corner. She was the only woman among ten or so addicts who were living in abominable circumstances under a few corrugated iron sheets.

Maria's second child was due in a few weeks' time. She knew we would take her to the maternity clinic – just as we had done with her first child. We saw her each week and regularly brought her food and clothing.

However, I didn't think she would readily come to Talita Cumi. Slowly the name Talita Cumi was becoming more widely known among the people on the street. At first, girls without children

came to us. They were a little older than the boys we usually took in. We set the limit between fifteen and thirty years of age. Gradually, a number of teenage mothers and their children came to live with us, like Georgia about whom we still know very little. Georgia had tried to commit suicide twice while living with us and that showed she was in great need of help. Her young daughter was with her when she tried the second time and said, 'Mummy, are you going to die again?' Little by little Georgia began to bond with her daughter and develop maternal feelings. This young woman was so confused. We hoped she would stay long enough to be able to really change.

Sara

It was not only girls from the street that were living with us. Sara was a twenty-one-year-old girl who started drinking because of a serious disease. She first used alcohol as a painkiller, but then became addicted to it. Sara was a pious Catholic and felt she always

had to give a good example at home, even when her parents got divorced. At that time, she was in her third year at the Higher

Agricultural College. Shortly after this, she started suffering from terrible abdominal pains. Because she couldn't keep any food down, she became so sick that all she could do was lie on her bed. The pains increased and tablets didn't help.

Even after an operation the pains didn't stop. A boyfriend forced her, against her own wishes, to drink alcohol and then she noticed the pains disappeared. That was the start of her addiction. In the end Sara, who was always so neat and tidy, was staggering down the street drunk. She was so ashamed about her drunkenness that one time she smashed a bottle in the street. But when she saw the alcohol gushing out of the bottle, the craving overwhelmed her, and she crawled down the street on her hands and knees to lick up the liquid. In this state of addiction, Sara came to Talita Cumi. For a long time she wasn't able to go back home, but she was doing very well. She freely admitted, 'One part of me wants to be here, another part wants to leave. Sometimes I don't know what to do. At times I behave very badly and at such moments I don't understand myself. But I know I am heading the right way. I used to read the Bible because that was tradition, as a kind of formula to get closer to God. But here I have learned that I need to reflect on it, word by word, so that it lodges in my heart. I know now that I can really talk with God and that He will make my dreams come true. The way up out of this valley is hard, but I know I will succeed. More than anything I am doing this for my mother.'

How I empathised with Sara. I recognised those abdominal pains so well. Those pains had been my monthly torment. Even major surgery and continuous use of medication had not brought a solution. Sometimes I was desperate. Thankfully, my condition is much better now, compared with how it was in the past. The last operation I had was done in Bolivia. I then realised that, as a foreigner, I was very privileged. I didn't have to stay in a basic hospital exposed to the risk of getting sicker. My gynaecologist was brother to one of the pastors in my church. He was excellent. And what genuine love I received from my Bolivian friends throughout my illness! They accompanied me to the operating theatre and were waiting for me when I came out. At one point, my room was too small for all the visitors!

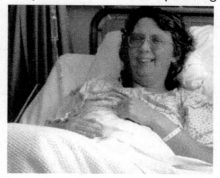

It is so good to be here, not only when I am sick, but every single day. My heart is in Bolivia. This has become my homeland.

I could talk to you about every girl in Talita Cumi. Each one of them had a story relating to abuse, rape, rejection, drugs and alcohol. On the one hand the stories were similar to those of the boys, on the other hand it was very different because they were

girls. I noticed that girls talked much more freely than boys. And they read more. Give them a Bible or a Christian book and they would sit reading for hours. With the boys, leafing through a cartoon was maybe the most they would do. But after having worked with men and boys for these many years, I had to get used to the fact that girls were less direct. They could say one thing and mean something else. For the all-female leadership team of Talita Cumi this proved very difficult. And team unity was harder to achieve and maintain.

The girls sometimes craftily played people off one against another. In order for us to become a good team, there was still a lot of work to be done.

Chapter 15

Dalma

I asked Dalma, one of the girls in Talita Cumi, to write down her story. Why Dalma? I want to show you that the gap between living as an ordinary decent citizen and life on the street is not as wide as you may think. One day Dalma looked down on the homeless, and the next day she was one of them. I discovered this thin line when I was working with the homeless in London at the age of nineteen. Many alcoholics came from a good background, but had ended up on the street because of a twist in the course of their life. Dalma, too, came from a normal family: her father was a trade union leader and she had a caring mother.

This is her story.

'Jorge had managed to rent a cheap flat where we often met to throw parties. Binge drinking and smoking cannabis were our ultimate leisure activities. For me the concept of leisure had a different meaning. Every day consisted of leisure time as I hardly ever spent any time on my studies. I was already rather tipsy when my friend Eve and I walked up the steps to Jorge's flat. With a giggle we responded to the loud voices of the lads. Each of us was lugging a heavy bag with bottles of strong drink up the steps. That evening I was paying for the drinks. The door of Jorge's flat was ajar. Most people were there already, some boys and girls who, like me, studied information technology, but also students from other faculties.

With a few exceptions they were all students from La Paz University. For us, getting drunk and smoking cannabis had become a way of life. We all had our own reasons to escape into drink and drugs. Tensions back home, study debts, disappointments in relationships, the bad prospects for the whole country or simply just to belong to the group. Discussions about the future or about the state of society invariably ended in drunken nonsense as the cannabis and alcohol took their toll and we all ended up falling asleep, only to waken later with splitting headaches. Taking to the bottle again was the only remedy for a hangover.

Despite our continuing drunken state, we still regarded ourselves as the intellectuals, too proud to admit that we were throwing away our future. Whenever I felt my own emptiness rising and was overwhelmed by that deep loathing of myself and my life, I would just take to the bottle. I was at my best when drunk. Then I could laugh, and cry, and show my emotions, but deep down I despised myself. I am by nature a quiet and shy girl, closed and a little distant.

For about a year, I had been thinking about ending it all. I couldn't cope with life any more. Always the pressure to succeed and endless questions from my parents or fellow students, 'When will you finish your studies? Have you taken any more exams?' I always just nodded and said nothing. I had stopped attending lectures long ago. The drink had got me in its grip. I was drinking non-stop.

It was no different that evening at Jorge's. By midnight most of the others were completely drunk, but I was still going strong. I left about 1am with Eve. It was June, so the winter night was quite cold, but we didn't feel it. We sat on the steps of the main post office in the centre of town, talking and drinking until finally I was so drunk that I fell asleep on the steps.

I woke with a shock and saw by the post office clock that it was three in the morning.

Where was Eve? I asked a passing security guard if he had seen my friend. He said that there had been no one with me for some time. I waited for half an hour: maybe she had gone to the loo and would return soon. But as time went on it began to dawn on me that I had been abandoned by my friend, here in the middle of this unsafe city.

What kind of friend is that? Is there anyone who really cares for me?

I forgot that my parents had always cared for me. Maybe they had cared too much. But dark thoughts began to rise in me like thunder clouds one after the other. I would no longer be welcome at home, no one would care if my life came to an end.

I got up and staggered through what would normally be the busy high street. It was empty and deserted apart from one or two homeless people. My thoughts were now turned to the plan that

had been on my mind for so long. I reached a conclusion. Now's the time to end it all. Why torment myself any longer with the endless craving for drink? It wasn't so far to the bridge over the river. Should I jump? No, the bridge is watched day and night, and if I'm caught my plan will not only fail, I'll have to pay a hefty fine for attempting suicide.

I decided to take the small alleyways and muddy paths down to the riverbank. It was about four thirty when I arrived at the bank. The white foam of the running water glistened in the moonlight. Looking up I saw the full moon above the snow-capped Mount Illimani, a magical scene, but one which only filled my heart with fear. I couldn't swim and just assumed the swift current would quickly take me down to my death.

Without further thought, I jumped into the ice-cold water, was swept down to the bottom and felt the river water rushing into me. But I constantly floated up to the surface and it seemed ages before I felt short of breath. Just at the moment I began to feel dizziness and blackness before my eyes, I panicked. Wildly thrashing around, I looked for something to grab hold of. I felt a tremendous urge to stay alive. It was as if I heard a voice within me saying, 'I don't want to die; I want to live!' Somehow, I managed to grasp a tree branch and to clamber out of the water and onto the branch. Shivering and dazed after my wild suicide attempt, I sat there for about half an hour.

Through the branches overhead, I could see Mount Illimani glowing pink in the rising sun. I started to cry and couldn't stop. Sobbing, I asked God to help me. It was so cold! I could hardly move my arms and didn't know how to get off the branch. I managed to creep on hands and knees towards the river bank. For more than an hour I fought to reach the edge. Once on the bank, I sat exhausted and shivering on a nearby bench.

A dog approached me and snuggled up to me as if he wanted to warm me up. Soon afterwards a boy dressed in rags appeared.

'What happened to you?' he asked.

I lied, 'I came here with some friends. They pushed me into the water, then left me here.'

'My name's Eusebio,' he said, shaking my hand, 'and my dog's called Optica.' It was his dog, then. It must have been seven thirty in the morning and the first sunrays danced through the tree branches hanging low over the river.

Soon about ten teenage boys and girls appeared, one gave me a jumper, another an old blanket, 'Put this on, you'll feel a bit warmer.'

I didn't feel good about this at first, thinking, 'Now they're being nice to me, but they'll rape and murder me soon.'

What did I know about them? They were homeless, and I'd always been told that you can't trust such people.

Even so, they seemed very different than I had expected. They took care of me as if I were one of their own. They gave me a llaucha, a sort of cheese pasty. I didn't want to accept it at first, but they insisted. I only took one bite, seeing that they were all so hungry. Slowly it began to dawn on me that my prejudice about these 'dirty, stinking tramps' was totally wrong. They were concerned about me, asking me where I lived. I lied, saying I had nowhere to live and had been abandoned by everyone. 'Then you can stay with us if you like,' offered Eusebio. He was sixteen and earned his money shining shoes. Thirteen-year-old Erwin earned money standing guard over cars at McDonalds. The youngest, Elvis, was twelve. I've forgotten the other names. They were not drunk or stoned.

'You're not going to hurt me, are you?' I asked.

'Don't worry. No one's going to hurt you, I'll take care of that,' said Eusebio. After a while I began to feel really thirsty. They offered me some alcohol mixed with water, but I didn't want it anymore. With their own money they bought me some Pepsi and insisted I drink it.

I didn't want to return home, having convinced myself that I would never be welcome again at my parents', that they would never have me back. I had refused their advice so many times, always going my own way. Whether my mother cried or pleaded, it had never made a difference to me.

Not to mention the state I was in, stinking to high heaven, bedraggled and dirty.

Then Eusebio said, 'Dalma, it's Thursday today, we always go to brother Juan's where we can shower and he gives us tea and bread. Do you want to come along?' I nodded and followed them towards the city centre. The streets were full of people going to work.

I pulled the jumper over my head so as not to be recognised by anyone I knew. When Eusebio saw that, he gave me his balaclava, without saying a word. Now I was one of them. I took Eusebio's hand and was aware of people looking at us. I had always looked down on these boys, or even turned my head away. I now saw how those people looked at me in just the same way. It made you feel rotten, like a piece of dirt, and you felt hatred rise within you against all the arrogance and prejudice, just because the other person happened to have a bit more luck than you did, and you happened to be poor.

We soon arrived at the Christian reception centre of brother Juan where many other homeless people were gathered. I was no longer the proud young woman I had been and began to talk to some of them for the very first time. Many told me how they spent their days and where they had a mattress for the night.

When one of the helpers came in, I saw how some people quickly concealed their bottles of drink. It was time to shower and no one wanted to be sent away because of the strict no-alcohol rule in the house. I wished I could have hidden myself away; it was awful to sit there and wait for the charity of others. At first, I didn't realise it was a Christian centre.

Before you could take a shower there was a sermon. One of the brothers, Dave, told us, 'Give your burdens to God and He will make them lighter. When you take them up again you will be able to carry them.' Those words touched me very deeply. I admitted to myself that I needed help, that I needed God's help. Earlier that day on the banks of the river, I had cried for His help for the first time.

I went over to brother Juan and asked if I could talk to him. He agreed but said I must shower first. Eusebio promised that he would stay around till after the talk. After the shower, I put my wet clothes on again. Then I told Juan my whole story, the suicide attempt, the addiction to alcohol. I cried and confessed to God my deep regret.

When I had calmed down a little, brother Juan encouraged me to call my parents, but I neither dared nor wanted to do that. I was so ashamed of myself. In the end Juan offered to call them himself and I agreed. He told me that they cried over the phone. He knew that the street was no place for me and said, 'You must wait here. Your mother will pick you up and she is bringing dry clothes for you.' After my talk with Juan I said goodbye to Eusebio, thanking him for his care for me. He had waited for me, even though Eve, my old friend, had abandoned me. I couldn't understand why these poor street people had been so kind to me. My world had been turned upside down.

While I was waiting for my mother, Juan told me of a newly-opened Christian centre for girls with the same problem as myself. 'But you can also go home with your mother and I will visit you every week,' he added. I thought to myself, 'If I go home with my mother nothing will change. It will be ok for a month or so, but then I'll fall back into the same old pattern.' So, I decided to go to the new house with the strange name, Talita Cumi. It was arranged within the hour. My mother had never expected this. She just wanted to take me home. 'Come on, you're sober now. Nothing's happened, and life can just go on,' she said.

But I insisted, 'Mum, I need help.'
My mother didn't understand at all, and said, 'You're all right, aren't you? That kind of house is no place for you. You're not homeless or on drugs, are you? You just drink a bit of alcohol. You're young, you'll get over it.'
Of course, she appreciated that my suicide attempt was no joke, so in the end she said, 'You're an adult, you must make your own decision.' I had made a sort of agreement with myself that if she had begun to cry, I would have gone home with her, but if she controlled her emotions I would go to Talita Cumi. I was surprised that she gave me the freedom to choose.

Chapter 16

New plans

In the meantime, we have also built a third stage house for our boys. That is the final stage before they go out into society independently. For a long time, these boys have lived in the same house alongside the newcomers: not an easy situation for the staff, or for the boys themselves. That problem has now been resolved when a wonderful facility has been built for these boys close to the other two houses. Juan and his wife Miriam moved in, so that they could parent the boys. Juan was deputy director of the whole work for some years.

Eventually, I will have to hand over more and more tasks to the Bolivian workers. Over the centuries the indigenous people have become dependent on white people in a way that is not good. Sometimes Bolivians appear very modest. I have noticed, however, that this is an impression. At times I think they are actually happy to let others get on with the work.

My job is to train a strong team that can work totally independently, both practically and spiritually. I realise this is difficult as long as I am involved, so I will have to distance myself increasingly from the daily management of the houses. I do want to maintain my regular contact with the people on the street, the homeless. I see so much need. I don't expect that during my lifetime homelessness will come to an end. The need is great. The work of Adulam is only a drop in the ocean. On the one hand that is frustrating, but on the other hand it motivates me to carry on. In 2003 the number of residents we could accommodate was about sixty: thirty boys and thirty girls and women.

The houses were fully occupied all the time. We were slowly rolling out the final stage provision for the boys. We also needed a similar final stage house for girls, but this plan was on hold.

I am regularly asked, 'Will you come back to The Netherlands when all the work has been taken over by the Bolivians?' I feel much too young to retire to The Netherlands. I actually think that I would rather stay here. I have come to love my friends dearly. And what about my children and grandchildren? How would I mange without Stephanie, and Carlos and Teresa, her father and mother? And then there are all the other boys and girls who look on me as their mother. I would miss my friends Beatriz and Teresa. I have become so fond of them. The church I attend has also become part of my life. Bolivia really is more my home country than The Netherlands. I would like to grow old here – but only if my Father in heaven agrees, of course.

Chapter 17

Dreams and miracles

The work among homeless and addicted people in La Paz grows and changes constantly; that is because of the people I am called to serve. In real life you encounter situations that require a practical solution. In this chapter I will recount a few initiatives that were born out of the needs of the people we were dealing with on a daily basis.

Marlene, the mother of three lovely children, asked me, when I met her on the street, 'When will you open a house for couples?' First I laughed a little and said, 'What do you mean, a house for couples? I don't have a money tree in the garden.'
But she persisted, 'Do you see that man over there? He is the father of my children. If I were to come with you, he would find himself a new girlfriend and I don't want that. If you had a house for couples, we could come together.'
I just listened to her and, without responding, I got back into the car. Without thinking, I turned the ignition key. The music CD restarted, 'Friends are friends forever, and a friend will not say never.' Then tears got the better of me. 'That is true,' I said to myself and to the people who were with me in the car. A spontaneous prayer went to the Lord, 'Lord, I cannot say "no" to this, but you will have to do a miracle again.'

In faith, we started to take steps. A piece of land was for sale in our area, and with some extra money that we had, we were able to purchase it. Then we had a conversation with our architect and started to seriously dream about the new house for couples. The name was born: Jesed (pronounced Chesed), meaning unconditional love, faithfulness and forgiveness. The plans were drawn up, but we didn't have much spare cash. It was really funny when the builder phoned me with the question, 'When are we starting?' I had a quarter of the money available because of a very unexpected and generous gift from England, so I asked him how much faith he had. That is how we started building. Little by little the funds came in, and when I stood in Jesed, I realised another miracle had taken place. Six couples were able to live with us.

In May 2009, we received the first two couples, among them Franklin and his wife Karina. Franklin was one of the first boys to come to Adulam. After being independent for a while, things had again gone wrong. He started selling cocaine and things went downhill fast. He met Karina, but often when he was high, he unleashed his anger and frustration on her. In those fights Karina suffered several severe wounds, but the wounds in her soul were even more devastating. Franklin and Karina were able to start a on new journey together. They were very grateful for the opportunity and worked really hard to make life changes. I am sure you can understand that opening a house to accommodate couples was a big challenge: a larger team, more people in our houses, new problems and also new opportunities to grow.

Another dream emerged as we grappled with the logistics of caring for mums who came to us with their children. We had always received them very lovingly in Talita Cumi.
During the daytime some of the children went to a local crèche,

but we could only enrol them once a year. Unfortunately, during the year we had various problems involving children, which caused difficulties for the other women and girls. We had to take action. So, we decided to make space available for day-care for our children in one of our houses known as Cecalab. That was a big step of faith, and was something we didn't expect to have to provide for a couple of years. The inner courtyard had to be covered to provide shelter from the sun. We had to plan a programme and recruit team members. The rooms, where

we welcomed the children and where they would find a safe place to play and develop normal social skills, had to be equipped.

I think about Esmeralda, who was almost two years old. She hadn't started to talk and needed help to develop on several different levels. Her mother, an 18-year-old girl, needed to learn to love and parent her child.

◆◆◆

We had developed an extensive programme for the rehabilitation of the boys and girls in our centres. We were able to get it printed to make it more widely available.

The title is: An educational therapeutic model providing teaching materials for learning life skills. In the book our whole programme was set out in detail, in such a way that others could also use it. I was privileged to present a workshop using our teaching materials at an international conference for rehabilitation centres.

Our residents learned new life skills in a creative way. For example, during a group session with the theme planning for the future, Vicky and Josefina had to complete a treasure hunt in our area. In the middle of the route there was a sweet, and at the end a chocolate bar. When they had gone nearly half way, they wanted to return to Talita Cumi.

But then they found the sweet. At this point, they discussed what to do, decided to carry on and finally also found the chocolate bar. Vicky's conclusion was this, 'You know Fineke, I actually do this often. I set out to do something, then I get fed up and throw in the towel. I never persevere. I understood today that, when I have set myself a goal, in spite of difficulties, I need to continue on till I have achieved what I want to do. I could do it today, so I can also achieve this in other circumstances.' I was moved to tears. Sure enough, when we do our part, the Lord will help us. Then we can achieve something that at first seemed impossible. We have seen this time and again in the lives of the young people in rehabilitation and we look forward expectantly to what lies ahead.

It was a rainy Christmas Eve, but that didn't stop us going out to meet up with our friends. As was our custom close to Christmas, we got ready to visit different street gangs to share a cup of hot chocolate with them and to tell them about the meaning of Christmas, when the Lord Jesus came to earth for us. We started off in obedience to the Lord and trusting that He would go before and watch over us.

Part of the team went ahead to the Ceja (the central point in El Alto). I stopped off with some staff to visit Doña Petrona, her children, grandchildren and others who were all living in the shack she calls home. In this cold and gloomy house, we were able to pray with people who were trapped in addictions and encourage them to put their trust in the Lord. After that we also went to the Ceja to join the rest of the team, under the bridge by the motorway. Gradually friends from different street gangs arrived and we had a good time talking together.

It was nearly midnight when, all of a sudden, a Mariachi band appeared. We had a laugh over how bizarre this was, because it was really unwise to be in this area without the protection we received from our friends. Then I saw there were three team members from Mision Adulam with the Mariachis: two, each with a lovely birthday cake, and one with a beautiful bunch of flowers. We sang with the Mariachis and danced in the street: it was a very special moment in honour of my birthday.

When the Mariachis had finished their performance, they quickly got themselves safely back into their vehicle and disappeared. This must have been the weirdest group of people they had ever played for.

I was honoured to cut the cake and to share the birthday celebration with all present. I shoved one cake under the seat of the jeep and put the other in front of me on the floor and started cutting. There was a lady with me who took the cake-filled plates from me. She then passed them on to the rest of the team waiting outside the vehicle. The team prepared to distribute the slices of cake to our friends.

The first slice provoked a reprimand, 'Not so big, otherwise there won't be enough.' A brother heard this and prayed very simply, 'Lord, let there be enough for everyone.' – and we all responded, 'Amen'. I kept on cutting the cake and after a while I asked how many more pieces we needed. I was told, 'Only for us who are serving', and I was able to distribute the rest, which was exactly enough for us.

As I stepped away from the car with my plate in my hand, I suddenly became aware that something totally impossible had happened. I had only cut one cake! We did a quick headcount of all the people present and came to a total of 92 people. The size of the cake I had cut usually served up to 38 people.

The Lord had done an amazing miracle of multiplication, without us being aware of it happening. The next day I cut the second cake and could only just produce 38 slices. Reflecting on this, we felt truly blessed because the Lord had participated in our celebration in the company of vulnerable, rejected and often invisible people. Just as in the Bible story, when the Lord made sure there was enough bread and fish for those who had nothing to eat, He made sure we could share our cake with all our friends!

Chapter 18

Moving on: 2022   Epilogue

It took quite some time and a lot of determination to get this book translated and ready for printing. As a result, a lot has happened since I last put pen to paper. Here is a short update about where we are now.

For eight years we reached out to addicted couples and, in Jesed, a total of fifty-eight couples benefitted from staying in this house. But then came the time when no more couples were looking for help. We went through an evaluation process, resulting in the closing of that project, while at the same time opening the doors of Jesed as a day centre with professional help for vulnerable children at risk.

For the last couple of years, we have been reaching out to several hundreds of children who have a variety of learning difficulties, as well as young teenagers who are starting to experiment with drugs. To help the latter group, we run an ambulatory rehabilitation programme and offer prevention classes in schools. In this way we reach many hundreds of young people who hopefully learn to stay away from taking drugs.

For the parents of the young people in our rehabilitation centres, as well as for those that come to Jesed, we offer courses to help them develop good parenting skills.

◆◆◆

As you know, in the early years I was heavily involved in prison ministry. Over the past few years, I have become more involved again and it is a privilege to visit people, listen to them and also preach in several different prisons. This is now possible because the Bolivian leaders in Misión Adulam are taking more responsibility, which frees me up for other areas of ministry. My changing role also gives me opportunities to speak and influence young people's lives in the local  church and to be involved in several ministries I have grown close to through the years.

◆◆◆

We continue to serve young people with addictions. In total, over one thousand young people have come through the doors of Adulam, Talita Cumi and Jesed. The problems have changed, although the drugs are still the same. We see a lot more teenagers who suffer with mental health issues. This means we need to personalise our ministry even more and cater for individual needs with the help of the professionals on the team.

We are deeply grateful for the people all over the world who help make this ministry possible. Through their faithful prayers and support, we serve our faithful God together!

Chapter 19

Burning questions

This book testifies to the grace and love of God. It was written primarily to encourage, motivate and inspire Christians.

Dear reader, as I said at the beginning, I hope you will ask yourself the big question, 'what can I, as a Christian, do in this world?' That is the purpose of this book.

There are people better-qualified and more suited for the work that I am currently doing in Bolivia. I am not especially strong and I didn't build up an amazing CV in The Netherlands. A Christian organisation thought it was too risky to employ someone who had suffered a nervous breakdown. I didn't have top marks in my Bible school diploma. In fact, I left for the mission field without any Bible school training. However, I am convinced that the Lord doesn't primarily look for all these things. He doesn't ask how capable we are, but He asks if we will trust Him: if we believe in His power, His love and His calling for our lives.

Maybe there are a few burning questions in your heart after reading this book. I try to recall a few I used to have myself. Then like me, you might wonder, 'Hey, I would like to do that; mission isn't as dull as I thought. Can I just spring into action? What should I do first?'

My answer might not be what you expected. The action starts at home!

First of all... don't run away from difficulties. Usually that means learning to get on with people you don't like very much, especially if these people are in leadership in your church. However imperfect your church leaders may seem to be, the church still provides the best training ground to learn to accept authority. Also, make a point of reading your Bible and praying regularly. If you don't cultivate these habits now, you are not going to learn them on the mission field. Remember, you take yourself with you everywhere you go.

It might be a sobering thought, but in the long run on the mission field the basics are the same as at home.

Here are some practical points. Witnessing isn't only talking about Jesus. If you are at school, you can be a witness by reacting in a positive way to things that happen in class. When your classmates disrespect a teacher, you don't need to join in. When there are fellow students who have problems or who are being bullied, you could befriend them and go home with them or invite to your house.

When you leave school and are wondering what to do next, ask yourself, 'How can I best serve the Lord?' You belong to the Lord and therefore your future career is the Lord's too. It is important to ask the Lord which profession to choose and which subjects to study.

You can seek God's guidance about holiday jobs. I worked for a while in a department store. These places also need people who know the Lord and can show the love of Jesus. I remember we had a customer in the store who was walking around with a bleeding finger. By offering this man a plaster, I did more than was expected. It may only be a small gesture, but it brings joy to people and warms their hearts. What is important is that you show what it means to be a Christian in your daily life through honesty, kindness, helpfulness and all the other qualities mentioned in the Scriptures the Lord has given us.

Maybe after reading this book, you think that the Lord can only use you after you have hit rock bottom, as happened to me. The Apostle Paul wrote in the Bible, '*When I am weak, I am strong*'. That doesn't mean you need to be weak to be strong. No, what this really means is that your strength comes from the Lord.

You don't need to be proud and rely on your own strength. Proud people can achieve a great deal in the world. But in the Lord's eyes, pride is a bigger problem than weakness. Pride is rebelling against the Lord. A weak person finds it easier to acknowledge that God is strong. In the Kingdom of God it is not a question of strength or weakness, but of simple dedication to the Lord. This is shown in the way in which you relate to Him on a daily basis, and the measure in which you allow Him to work through you.

Maybe you think that weakness means you just wait passively to see what comes your way. No, that is just laziness. In some ways faith can be compared with professional sporting achievements. What counts in sport is training, fitness and perseverance. You have to work hard to reach your goal. There are many scriptures that show the importance of perseverance. If you think that, after your conversion, God will organize everything for you, you are wrong. Conversion isn't a one-off event; it is a way of life. You need to turn away constantly from pride, laziness and the natural inclination to make wrong choices. Perseverance builds character.

Paul made a comparison between Christians and sportsmen for a reason. *(1 Cor 9: 24-27)* It is a life of self-denial, persistence and training to obtain the prize. There are a lot of things I don't understand, and I sometimes wonder why certain things go on for so long before they change. But I know that the Lord doesn't waste a day or an hour of our lives on things that are not necessary. Perseverance and patience are a normal part of the Christian's walk with God. If you choose to slacken the pace, then you might arrive at the finishing line after the organizers of the competition have already put the banners away and the supporters have gone home. Perhaps only your own family would still be waiting for you to give you a lift home. Or you can train and prepare in such a way that you arrive at the finishing line in good time.

I agree that our progress isn't only influenced by our own attitudes, but also by the support of those around us. You need the encouragement of a mentor. Maybe I would never have made it to the mission field if my pastor hadn't stood by me so faithfully. We need to encourage one another to continue walking with the Lord and make the most of all the opportunities He gives us.

There are ways to prepare to be a faithful disciple of Jesus for the rest of your life.

First of all, you need to set yourself a goal, after seeking guidance from the Lord. You need to be prepared to bring everything in line with that goal.

Secondly, it is necessary that you are very clear about your commitment to that goal. The Bible says, *'Let your yes be yes, and your no, no'*. Unfortunately, nowadays this golden rule is often ignored. You can see this in married couples when their 'Yes', after some years, can all of a sudden become 'No'. With God that is impossible. God said 'Yes' to me and He will never break His promise. He is not going to come to the conclusion, at some point in my life, that He is fed up with me. No, He will complete the work that He has started. God is the author and finisher of our faith. This same attitude is expected of us as Christians.

Thirdly, you need to be prepared to give it your all. When people want to go to an international football match, they are prepared to pay a fortune. They have to make a long journey, sometimes half way round the world. They will stand in endless queues, have to go through all sorts of security checks and then run the risk of finding themselves in the midst of fighting hooligans. Christians can sometimes grumble over trivial things, for example when a church service continues longer than expected, showing they are not prepared to invest significantly in their faith. What is most important in your life? Are you willing to give up everything for it?

Fourthly, you need to be obedient. Part of being a disciple of Jesus is that you are aware that your conversion is a covenant that God made with you, to which you have said 'Yes'. You have become a follower of the Lord Jesus and need to trust that His plans and thoughts about you are good. Then you need to get to know these plans and thoughts. You need to train in obedience and trusting the Lord.

How do you do that? When we read the Bible, the Lord reveals Himself and shows us what He wants of us. If you choose not to read the Bible, you will not know what He has to say and you will not fully experience a living relationship with Him. 'Being a disciple of Jesus' and 'having a relationship with God' might sound vague, but the reality is very practical. It means that you look around you and offer help to the people the Lord brings across your path. At home or at work, where people know you inside out, is the best training ground for learning to be a disciple of Jesus. Serving God isn't something high and unattainable. It means practising Biblical values in daily life. You may help someone who is ill or disabled. You are honest in all your dealings and you give without expecting anything in return.

When you simply put into practice the principles of the Bible in everyday life, you'll find you will be growing in your faith and commitment. Faith is not merely doing a succession of good deeds in your own strength. No! You will soon find out that doing good doesn't come naturally, but is only possible when you stay close to the Lord and are filled with the Holy Spirit. That is the key to a joy-filled life. This reminds me of the scripture I was given at confirmation: *'May the God of hope fill you with all joy and peace as you trust in Him, so that you may overflow with hope, by the power of the Holy Spirit.' (Romans 15:13)*

Printed in Great Britain
by Amazon

12770877R00092